Narrative Design
The Craft of Writing for Games

Michael Breault

CRC Press
Taylor & Francis Group
Boca Raton London New York

CRC Press is an imprint of the
Taylor & Francis Group, an **informa** business

CRC Press
Taylor & Francis Group
6000 Broken Sound Parkway NW, Suite 300
Boca Raton, FL 33487-2742

International Standard Book Number-13: 978-0-367-19153-5 (Hardback)
International Standard Book Number-13: 978-0-367-19152-8 (Paperback)

Library of Congress Cataloging-in-Publication Data

Names: Breault, Michael, author.
Title: Narrative design: the craft of writing for games / by Michael Breault.
Description: Boca Raton, FL: CRC Press, 2020. | Includes bibliographical references and index.
Identifiers: LCCN 2019052439| ISBN 9780367191535 (hardback) | ISBN 9780367191528 (paperback) | ISBN 9780429200762 (ebook)
Subjects: LCSH: Games—Design and construction. | Narration (Rhetoric)
Classification: LCC GV1230 .B74 2020 | DDC 794.8/1535—dc23
LC record available at HYPERLINK "https://protect-us.mimecast.com/s/ewoMCDkY05iBBDPj5u5wuuq?domain=lccn.loc.gov" https://lccn.loc.gov/2019052439

Visit the Taylor & Francis Web site at
http://www.taylorandfrancis.com

and the CRC Press Web site at
http://www.crcpress.com

Narrative Design

For Mary, always

Contents

Acknowledgements

Many thanks to my stalwart reviewers: Mary Breault (as always, my first editor), Chris Breault, Adam Cogan, and James Macanufo.

Author

Mike Breault has worked in the game industry since 1984 as a narrative designer and game designer. He has helped create more than 90 analog games and 40 digital games. In 2014, he began teaching narrative design and game design to college students at several universities. Mike has a B.S. in Physics and an M.A. in Instructional Design. He currently teaches in Webster University's Games and Game Design program. He and his wife, Mary, live in St. Louis, MO.

Courtesy of Ava Vikman and Webster University.

Introduction

ABOUT ME

Before you devote the time and effort to reading a book, you should know who wrote it. I've been in the game industry for 35 years now. In that time, I've worked on over 90 analog games (board games, card games, and tabletop role-playing games) and just under 40 computer and video games. I started at TSR back in 1984, working on Dungeons & Dragons® and Advanced Dungeons & Dragons® games and adventures, board games, hardback books, and card games, over 90 of them in all. I co-designed my first computer game, *Pool of Radiance*, in 1987. I left TSR in 1989 to go freelance and have worked on digital games almost exclusively ever since, though I've recently returned to working on analog games. I've worked as both a narrative designer and a game designer, often both on the same project. For a list of my publications, see Appendix A.

For the last few years, I've been teaching narrative and game design at several universities, currently at Webster University in St. Louis. The courses I create and teach are based on the tasks narrative designers and game designers perform every day during game development. I want students to get a real look at the work they'd be doing as writers and designers in the game industry. It's exciting to witness the creativity and enthusiasm students bring to these assignments. This book will help instructors and students learn more about game design and narrative design. Those already in the industry can use this book to hone their skills in these disciplines.

I'm often asked how I got into the game industry. I always say I owe it all to the Chicago Cubs, which garners me some startled looks. Here's how it happened. I went to college for physics and astronomy and made my way into the Ph.D. program in astrophysics at Indiana University. After a few years there, I realized that astronomy wasn't for me and I wasn't for it. Searching for a career that suited me, I left to work as an editorial intern at a local political opinion magazine (*The American Spectator*). That magazine had an annual Chicago Cubs outing. My wife and I went, stayed overnight in Chicago, and got the *Sunday Tribune* the next morning. Mary spotted an ad for a game editor at TSR (the makers of *Dungeons & Dragons*®). I applied for the job, got it, and was on my way. So, yeah, the Chicago Cubs started me out in the game industry.

Your career can take some strange turns, as mine amply demonstrates. Be open to interesting paths, as you never know where they might lead.

ABOUT THIS BOOK

My experiences as a narrative designer, game designer, and college professor form the basis for this book. I'd like to pass along the lessons I've learned over the years to anyone who's interested in writing and designing games. This book serves as a practical introduction to these crafts. We'll examine what narrative designers do as well as how and why they do it. We'll explore the collaborative nature of game design and see how writers and designers interact with everyone else on the team during the development process. The nuts and bolts of this work is contained in the assignments in Appendix C.

We won't be discussing narrative philosophies, narratology vs. ludology, or other issues that belong in the realms of theory and academia. This book concentrates on practical matters, not theoretical ones. Plenty of other books focus on the latter. Here we'll help readers develop the skills and creative works they need to enter the game industry or improve upon the abilities they already have.

While much of the content of this book deals with designing and writing for digital games, aspects of working on analog games are also covered. Sections of some chapters will compare writing work in the digital and analog realms. The exact process often differs, but the work designers and writers do in those two distinct game industries is closely related. Chapter 10 focuses entirely on the narrative and design tasks specific to analog games.

INTENDED AUDIENCES

- **For Students:** Students can use this book to supplement the information their own instructors pass along. The content of each chapter conveys foundational knowledge about game design and narrative design, while the assignments in Appendix C give students the opportunity to combine that knowledge with their own ingenuity to showcase their design skills.

- **For Instructors:** Teachers of college and high school game design and narrative design classes can use this book as an invaluable resource for their classes and students. The information in the chapters provides supplemental content students can absorb on their own, while the class syllabi in Appendix B can be used to build or refine classes in game design and narrative design. The assignment instructions and templates included in Appendix C provide teachers with ready-made assignments designed to bring out their students' creativity. Many of the assignments are collaborative: teamwork is key in nearly all game development efforts.

- **For New and Current Game Designers and Narrative Designers:** Anyone looking to break into the game industry will find plenty of advice ahead. Each chapter gives detailed information about one or more aspects of game development. Appendix C contains assignments and templates to help develop the pieces of a portfolio that will attract the attention of game companies. I've been involved in a lot of hiring decisions over the years (both as an interviewer and an interviewee) and I know what game companies look for.

- For those already in the game industry, the information and assignments in this book can help them expand and refine their portfolio to improve their chances of advancing their careers.

- **For Fans of Games:** This book should also interest those looking at the game industry not as a career but as an intriguing new field employing hundreds of thousands of people all over the world. How the game industry works and how games are made should become clear as you read this book.

CHAPTER 1

What Is Narrative Design?

WRITER VERSUS NARRATIVE DESIGNER

A narrative designer is a writer embedded in a game development team. The word "embedded" is critical. A contractor who has been hired for a month or two to work remotely at the end of a project to polish the dialogue is not really a narrative designer. They are a script doctor called in at the end to dot the *i*'s and cross the *t*'s. A narrative designer is integral to the team and project, from the first concept to publication. A narrative designer has tremendous influence on the game's story and how it meshes with gameplay to deliver the intended player experience. To do this work properly, you need to be there with the rest of the team from start to finish.

Think of a narrative designer as a writer who also does game design and whose work intersects with that done by everyone else on the game dev team. Or think of a narrative designer as a designer who writes. At times in this book, I may use "writer" and "narrative designer" interchangeably, mostly for variety's sake.

It's all just terminology anyway. Different companies refer to the position by a variety of names. My official titles have varied among narrative designer, writer, game writer, designer, game designer, story designer, senior narrative designer, senior game designer, lead narrative designer, and more. There's no standard way to refer to this position, just as there's no standard set of tasks that fall within this person's bailiwick.

It all depends on the company you're working for, the team and project you're on, and the needs of all three.

Unlike a writer who creates a novel or a movie script, a narrative designer needs to wear a multitude of hats (as do many other game developers). Thinking of yourself as a designer who writes helps you realize that a lot of your work is game design with an overlay of writing tasks. Many times, especially in smaller companies and smaller teams, the narrative designer is just whoever on the team writes best. That person might be primarily a game designer, sound designer, programmer, animator, artist, creative director (CD), etc., but on top of those duties they take on the writing tasks of a narrative designer.

Also unlike writers in other media, narrative designers are creating interactive experiences in which players are active participants. The linearity of story that exists in other media goes out the window (or it should) when you add player agency into your story. That requires a more flexible approach to the story-creation process.

As a narrative designer, you'll do a lot of document writing during the pre-production stage of a game's development. The writing you do at this stage will be a reference for the team throughout development and will help determine both the game's tone and structure. During production, not only will you be writing dialogue and in-game text, you'll often find yourself doing scripting and other design-oriented tasks. And you'll be interacting with virtually every member of the team, as the game's story affects every aspect of the game; it informs every decision and every action taken by the team.

We'll talk about developers and design teams later in this book, including the many ways narrative designers interact with the other members of the team. But for now, let's look at what the narrative designer does on their own.

NARRATIVE DESIGN

If narrative design is what narrative designers do for a living, what does that entail? A lot of things, as it turns out.

We can sort a narrative designer's tasks into three buckets:

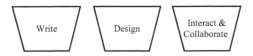

Writing

All the writing that goes into a game falls squarely on the narrative designer's shoulders. This encompasses not only all the dialogue and text the player might see in the game, but also all the story elements that go into the development of the game. These often serve simply to inform various members of the team as they create art, animation, gameplay, world design, and so on.

Oftentimes the narrative designer is assigned (or volunteers for!) many of the pre-production writing tasks necessary to create a solid design foundation for the implementation stage, when the game is actually created. These tasks include the concept document, game design document, level or zone design documents, scripts for presentations to upper-level management, and any other writing the team needs during pre-production.

Once production begins, the narrative designer begins writing character dialogue, text for notes and books placed in the game, and other writing-related tasks. Often, scripters and game designers place first-draft versions of dialogue lines into the game, ensuring that they convey gameplay-related content at appropriate times. It's the narrative designer's job to find and edit all those lines, making sure they fit the tone of the game and the character speaking.

On many projects, a game development team will have a single narrative designer but a dozen or more others (scripters, game designers, level designers) adding dialogue and story-related content into every area of the game. Ideally, the narrative designer can track all the lines that have been added to the game (or modified) by others, and serves as the final set of eyes on every bit of writing that goes in. As the project nears a deadline, the team often adds content at a furious pace, and the narrative designer has to dash from one part of the script to another to put out all the fires.

Writing cinematic scripts is another of the narrative designer's responsibilities. These mini-movies are scattered throughout most games, at the start, end, and at various turning points in the plot. Game development teams use cinematics to convey story, events, or information that is difficult or impossible to present during gameplay. They can be mini-movies, like the cinematic of the player's plane crashing at the start of *Bioshock*, or semi-interactive set pieces, like the elevator ride into the underwater city of Rapture a few minutes later—both have narration that establishes the themes of the game, written by narrative designers. (More on cinematic scripts in the narrative design assignments in Appendix C.)

Games change dramatically during production. The opening level of the first *Red Faction* game was thrown out and completely redone with only three weeks left until the game's release. During production of the second *Red Faction* game, an entire level (1/13th of the game) was deleted with only a couple of months to go, as we realized we didn't have time to finish it. Cinematic scripts can change dramatically as well. The first drafts of a game's cinematic scripts are often created during pre-production and later rewritten to accommodate changes to the story and gameplay. Sometimes just an outline of the anticipated content of a cinematic is written up during pre-production, with the full version created once the game's story and design fall into place.

As the game solidifies during production, and the story and gameplay information cinematics need to convey to the player become better known, more complete versions of cinematic scripts can be written. These are reviewed by the creative director and the leads of other disciplines within the development team. That feedback spurs further refinement of the scripts.

Once the cinematic scripts are approved by the CD and leads, a concept artist creates storyboards to block out the action within each cinematic. These are reviewed and revised until leads are satisfied with them. Then the cinematic team goes to work creating the first prototype of the cinematic, with the narrative designer contributing feedback and rewrites as needed. The team continues to refine the cinematics in subsequent passes until they are approved by all concerned.

If a game has spoken dialogue, the narrative designer faces a few more challenges. A voice recording script must be created near the end of production. This means gathering the thousands or tens of thousands of dialogue lines into scripts organized by character. The lines of each character—no matter where they appear in the game—should be grouped into a single document or spreadsheet. These documents provide context to help the voice actor with their lines—voice actors often have to imagine their character's situation without access to the game itself. Each cinematic in the game also needs its own voice recording scripts (one for each voice actor) with each character's lines highlighted.

Once the voice recording scripts are finalized, the narrative designer is off to a recording studio to help guide the voice recording sessions, usually alongside a voice director and an audio technician. The technician handles the mechanical process of recording and saving multiple takes of each line, and the voice director listens for speech issues. The narrative designer's part is to guide the voice actors' delivery and determine which take of a line to use in the game, as no one knows the emotional and gameplay context of the game's dialogue like the narrative designer.

When the recording sessions are over, the team's sound designers work to get the approved lines into the game. The narrative designer then needs to play the game, listen to the voice lines, and call out any that are playing incorrectly or have other problems.

There are often pickup sessions built into the audio schedule, much like "reshoots" for studio films. These occur weeks later, to re-record any bad lines or account for places where the game has changed, making the original line irrelevant. As few voice actors as possible are called back to the studio to record new or revised lines. These sessions are expensive but are almost always necessary to ensure top-quality dialogue for a game.

Designing

Much of a narrative designer's work falls within the realm of game design. During pre-production, when the foundation for development is being laid, the narrative designer is often tasked with writing the game design document, creating the initial versions of level or zone design docs, and breaking down the story into specific events, settings, and situations the player will encounter in the game. These design tasks are so closely intertwined with the game's story that the narrative designer is usually the team member best suited to writing these documents.

Once production starts, narrative designers find themselves taking on scripting tasks related to the game's story. These include getting characters into the game and scripting their interactions with each other and the player, writing notes and brief texts for the player to find and read in-game, and implementing dialogue to help convey the game's story to the player. Most game development teams have a squad of designers dedicated to scripting, so the narrative designer usually tackles scripting work that involves dialogue and characters with whom the player can interact.

Interacting and Collaborating

Everyone on a game development team interacts with everyone else on that team. This interpersonal collaboration is how game development gets done. Since the game's story affects every other aspect of its development, narrative designers end up interacting with most members of the team on a daily basis. They talk with game designers about how the story, characters, and events will be implemented into the game. They talk with character artists about the characters created from the descriptions the narrative designer wrote. They discuss the game's soundscape with the team's sound designers. They similarly interact with all other members of the team, in every discipline, sometimes multiple times a day.

In my own experience, you spend about one-third of each day on a game project interacting with other team members. You might notice that a dialogue line isn't playing correctly in a certain part of the game, and you go to talk to a scripter or sound designer about it. Or you might gather around a cinematic artist's chair with others to watch the latest version of the opening cinematic. Whether discussing a particular issue with another developer, brainstorming with a group, or gathering in an impromptu session to talk about the game and its progress in general, these interactions are powerful engines that drive the game's development forward.

Over my years in the game industry, I slowly realized the importance of these personal connections. Not only is getting up from your chair and walking over to talk with someone the best way to iron out problems, it also helps build your network of personal connections in the industry. An issue that's easily communicated in person might offend or confuse a colleague if you state it bluntly over email or even a more casual team platform like Slack. When I was working on the *Wolfenstein* 2009 game, I noticed that as I fired an automatic rifle at a spot on a wall, it made a perfect circle around where the cursor was aimed instead of a random scattering of bullet holes. Dragging a slightly irritated programmer over to my desk and showing this to him conveyed the problem much better than any email could. I gradually learned to get up and talk to people directly to avoid miscommunication. This personal touch can contribute to your career success in astonishing ways.

These interactions and collaborations require narrative designers (and everyone else on a game team) to develop soft skills. We'll talk more about these skills in Chapter 7, but for now let's just say these are the people skills that enable us to work together as a team, talk our way through differences, compromise to achieve common goals, and pull in the same direction for the good of the project. Many developers struggle with these soft skills in their careers; it's not unusual for them to take time and effort to improve. Any time you have a negative interaction with a fellow team member, view it as an opportunity to reflect and develop your soft skills.

NARRATIVE DESIGN TASKS

Here's a list of tasks that often fall into a narrative designer's lap. Which of these you will have to handle depends on your skills and the needs of the project.

Create design documents	Work with animators
Be the CD's point person	Work with engineers
Brainstorm	Work with localization
Maintain CD's vision	Work with sound designers
See the whole game	Temporarily record dialogue
Write the game's story	Help choose voice actors
Create characters	Direct voice sessions
Write dialogue	Pick the best version of each line
Write cinematic scripts	Ensure correct voice-over (VO) lines are in-game
Work with designers	Script
Work with artists	Playtest

Each of the above tasks has its own revision cycle. An initial version of the work is created. It gets reviewed by the CD and relevant discipline leads, their feedback is incorporated into the next iterations of the work, and then the work gets placed into the game. At that point, other developers on the team and members of the QA team (Quality Assurance—playtesters) provide feedback. This drives further cycles of revision. Focus groups and outside testers give suggestions that help refine the work even further.

We'll look at the narrative designer's work in more detail later in this book. For now, glance at the above list again and you'll spot a couple of general trends. One is that a multitude of design tasks fall to the narrative designer. Those who fill this position should truly think of themselves as designers as well as writers. Another trend is that much of a narrative designer's job involves interacting with other members of the team. Writing and design aren't the only skills a narrative designer needs to learn; the soft skills outlined in Chapter 7 are right up there in importance to your game development career.

CHAPTER 2

What Is Game Design?

Now let's talk about the basics of game design. Game design and narrative design are so tightly intertwined that this book will cover aspects of each discipline, as well as the interactions between them.

There are a variety of ways to think about game design. Here are three of the ways I describe game design in my classes. At least one of these should resonate with you to help guide and inform your design work.

GAME DESIGN DEFINITION #1

Game design is the art of crafting the player experience.

Let's break that down a bit.

First off: Let's not argue about whether game design is an art or not. As far as I'm concerned, any creative activity undertaken by an intelligent creature counts as art. If that doesn't mesh with your definition of art, that's all right. Just stick with me for a minute.

Game design is also a craft. It's a skill that you learn only with a lot of practice and with plenty of help from those better at it than you. There's certainly an apprentice → journeyman → master hierarchy in game design. Many companies explicitly state this in their employee rankings. I've seen several companies with categories of junior designer, designer, senior designer, and lead designer. Others give levels to this (and other) disciplines, wherein those new to design start as Level 1 Designers and can work their way up through the ranks (over the course of a decade or more) to Level 5 Designers.

When HR brings you to your seat on your first day of work, to the left of you may be a woman who has been doing your job for 20 years now. To your right might be a man who's been doing it for ten years. You're going to learn more from them in the next three months than you learned in four years of college courses. That's why game design is a craft—you learn by doing, and by doing it alongside others more experienced than you.

The most important element of this first definition, though, is the part about the player experience. That determines everything about a game's design. What do you want players to get out of your game; what's the experience you want them to have? Once you define that experience, every aspect of your game design should work toward delivering it. Build your story hooks and gameplay mechanics around that ideal player experience.

GAME DESIGN DEFINITION #2

Game design is answering the journalist's questions for your game.

Every article a journalist writes should answer six one-word questions— Who? What? How? Why? Where? and When? Answering those questions about the article's topic enables the reporter to give readers a complete picture of the issue at hand.

These guiding questions can be used in game design as well as in the fields of journalism and research, to give game designers a complete picture of their game's overall intent and direction. Here's how game designers should ask those questions:

Who is my game for?
Carefully considering this question makes you think about the target audience for your game. Who are your players?

What do they want/expect from this type of game?
Once you've identified the target audience for your game, you need to understand what they want when they play your type of game. Who plays this type of game, and what have they enjoyed about previous games in this genre? (A corollary: Come up with ways to surprise your players with twists that deviate from genre expectations.)

How *am I going to fulfill those desires and expectations?*
Now that you've found your audience and decided what they want, you need to figure out how to provide it. What mechanics will give them the desired experience? What new system can we add that will bring something fresh to the genre, without compromising the core appeal?

Why *did I choose this game system/mechanic? Why is this mechanic in my game?*
Once you've outlined the mechanics that will deliver the player experience, step back and think about each one. What is it adding to the overall experience? Does it mesh well with the other game mechanics? Are there ways it could work better? Ask these questions about every mechanic in the game and do it at multiple points during the game's development. Ideas that worked well at the start of production may need to be left by the wayside as the shape and style of the game changes.

Imagine that you originally incorporated a fast means of traveling around your game world, such as a jetpack. But after you build the world, you watch playtesters blast through it at high speed, landing only at the areas that look most interesting, and then complaining that the world is too small. The easiest solution is to remove the jetpack. Now players move slower and see more of your world, stopping at all the interesting spots that used to be flyover country.

Identifying these issues as soon as possible, before the team spends more resources iterating on them, is essential. As the game changes, keep asking why each feature exists!

Where *is my game being delivered to customers?*
What platforms are you creating your game for? This greatly affects your feature set and user interface, as well as considerations about your audience. Players on mobile platforms have very different sets of expectations from those who play on consoles or PCs. This is a fundamental aspect of your game design plans and should be settled very early on.

When *is my deadline for delivery?*
This is your project's due date. While it may seem unrelated to the design of your game, it's actually critical to development. Game production schedules work their way backward from the game's publication date. If it's going gold on this date, it needs to be ready for final polishing a few months earlier, it needs to go into playtesting three months before that,

and all voiced lines need to be in the game a month before that, and so on, back to the very start of development. While smaller teams may now plan an "Early Access" release on digital platforms that gives them room to refine the game, even then you must stick to a schedule for releasing content (or else face the wrath of user reviews).

The time you get to complete and polish each stage of the game flows from the delivery date you set at the start of the project. Games do miss delivery dates, but the initial planning for the development stages of your game is all dependent on that final delivery date.

GAME DESIGN DEFINITION #3

My final definition of game design revolves around an Internet meme—Honey Badger. If you're not familiar with this character or have only distant memories of him, visit YouTube and search for "Honey Badger." Click on the three-minute video narrated by Randall. Listen for the refrain that encompasses Honey Badger's outlook on life—"Honey Badger doesn't give a shit."

Courtesy of flikr.com.

Think of your player as Honey Badger. Honey Badger doesn't give a shit how hard you worked on your game, how much it cost, how many hours you devoted to it, how smart your parents think you are, or how good you think your game is. Honey Badger doesn't give a shit about any of that.

All Honey Badger cares about is their experience playing your game. Is it fun? Is it challenging? Is it engaging? Is it worth the money I paid for it? Is it worth the time I've invested in it? Those are the things Honey Badger cares about. If you don't meet most or all of those expectations, Honey Badger is going to be unhappy. Honey Badger is going to go online and yell about your game on social media.

> *My third definition of game design is that it's the art of making Honey Badger give a shit.*

If you can make that ornery, hard-to-please Honey Badger player care about your game, then you've succeeded as a game designer.

In my classes, after I explain this definition, I hand out wrist bracelets with "WWHBT?" embossed on them—What Would Honey Badger Think? I tell students to wear the bracelets or keep them around when they're creating games, to remind them of that hard-to-satisfy player as they design. Many of my students wear these bracelets to class and tell me that they really do help them think more about the player as they design their games.

PUTTING IT ALL TOGETHER

Perhaps you noticed the one element common to all three of the above definitions of game design—the player. Always keep the player in mind and think of the experience you're creating for them. Who is your player, what do they want, and how are you going to deliver that experience? Keep those questions at the forefront of your mind as you design.

GAME SYSTEMS AND GAME MECHANICS

These two elements of game design are critical to the construction of your game. Game systems are the "what?" of game design—what can the player do in the game? Think of them as the player verbs of your game. Game mechanics are the "how?" of your design—how exactly do those game systems work? Game mechanics are detailed explanations of your game systems.

Game systems are the large-scale aspects of your game—combat, movement, the game world, puzzle-solving, character generation, interactions with NPCs (non-player characters, the people and creatures that inhabit the world the player is exploring). These are the elements of game design that come directly from the designer's decisions about the sort of game they want to create for players.

Game systems are the easy part. Game mechanics are where it really gets messy. You say you want players to be able to create their own unique characters in the game? How does that work, exactly? What races, classes, statistics, abilities, and progression will you design into your character creation system? And how does each of those work? You'll need to define every aspect of your game mechanics in painful detail.

Your game has combat? Great, but how does that work exactly? What player character (PC) stats relate to everything PCs can do in battle? What combat subsystems will you have—melee, ranged, magic, psionics, ship-to-ship combat? And how does each of those work? You can make an initial pass at the game systems that will be allowed in your game in a day or less, but the game mechanics that govern those systems will take you weeks to work out. That's where game design really happens.

Periodically you need to critically evaluate each system and mechanic in your game. (Remember the "Why?" question in my second definition of game design above.) Systems and mechanics that fit your earlier thoughts on gameplay can end up no longer working well with the rest of your design. The sooner you realize this and adjust, the smoother your project will go.

FLOW AND PROGRESSION

A final game design idea involves maintaining a *flow state* in players. A flow state is a feeling of intense engagement with an activity. The phrase was coined in the mid-1970s by a Polish researcher, Mihály Csíkszentmihályi, who studied the intense focus that artists exhibited when immersed in their work. His studies found that across different activities, as the level of challenge and the skill of the participant increased, so did the participant's sense of immersion.

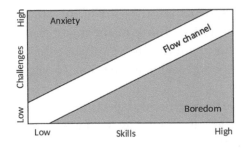

Courtesy of Psychology Today.

As shown in the chart above, there's an optimal zone of correlation between an activity's level of challenge and the participant's skill level. Ensuring that the challenge rises with the skill level keeps the participant in a flow state of maximum engagement with the activity.

If a game's challenge level rises faster than the player's skill (mastery of the game mechanics), then the player's progress in the game grinds to a halt. Frustration and anxiety increase, and the player starts to feel like throwing the controller at the screen or flipping over the game board. On the other hand, if the player's skill level overwhelms the challenges the game poses, boredom and a desire to play other games results.

A player's flow state is linked closely with the game's progression. Game designers need to ensure that the challenges posed by the game keep pace with the player's growing mastery of the game's mechanics. As the PC gains new skills and better equipment, the monsters they fight need to get tougher and more numerous. This need for progression affects every aspect of a game's design, from the items the player can find, buy, or make, to the PC's rise in ability as they gain experience, to the foes the PC faces as they progress through the game.

This is a balancing act that continues throughout a game's development. The designers need to aim for the midpoint of their expected audience, hoping to provide an engaging level of challenge for as many players as they can for as long as they can. One danger during development is that the Quality Assurance (QA) team—the internal playtesters—get so used to the gameplay that almost no level of challenge is too hard for them. This has led to games getting so hard that external playtesters can't handle them, triggering the development team to ratchet down the difficulty to a realistic level.

Game design is an intricate mix of intent, work ethic, evaluation, and revision. Intent informs and drives your design, but hard work and creativity turn intentions into reality. You need to constantly evaluate every element of your game's design to ensure it's still working to deliver the intended experience. These evaluations tell you what needs fixing or removing, which pushes your own game design skills to improve every day.

CHAPTER 3

Story in Games

WHAT IS A STORY?

Every game has a story. That story is the foundation that gives context to the players' actions. Good game stories empower players with agency, enabling them to drive the story forward. It lets them know where they fit into the game world and what their goals are in the game.

A game's story doesn't have to involve any writing, dialogue, or text. Chess is an abstract strategy game with a story. Two kingdoms meet on a battlefield. Each king has troops to fight for him, and each side's goal is to capture the opposing king. The names and shapes of the pieces—knights, pawns, bishops, king, queen—are evocative of the historical origins of chess. That story gives context for chess players; the goal conveyed by that story informs every action players take in that game, whether they realize it or not.

Courtesy of libreshot.com.

The story for *Monopoly* is equally simple. Each player is a wheeler-dealer in the real estate world of Atlantic City. Players strive to corner the market on the city's properties and bankrupt all their rivals. Last player standing is the city's new real estate mogul. That story and end goal drive every player's activities in *Monopoly*.

A game's story isn't something that gets in the way of gameplay. And it shouldn't be set up with a wall of text from some second-string character, like the village elder at the start of a fantasy adventure. At its most basic, a game's story forms a background for gameplay and gives context to players that helps motivate them to continue to play. In a well-developed game, story enhances gameplay and never gets in the way of players' enjoyment of the game.

Think of *Shadow of the Colossus*. It's an action game about a young man fighting 16 giant monsters in a forbidden land. The script is short on dialogue—large stretches of the game, including the first five minutes, are wordless. Yet players and critics view it as one of gaming's greatest adventures and fondly remember the protagonist and his horse. By limiting dialogue and explanation, *Shadow of the Colossus* establishes a deep sense of mystery and foreboding. Its script does more with less.

STORY IN GAMES

In a video game, stories serve several purposes:

Stories give context for players, grounding them in the game's fiction and world. They tell players what the game is about, what part they play in the story, and what they are supposed to do in the game. This helps engage players in the game world.

Stories motivate players to continue by intriguing them with what's around the next corner. One of the primary goals of a game's story is to lead players on with mysteries, subplots, and engaging characters. Games with more complex stories will have a rolling collection of subplots, with new ones opening up as old ones are resolved, to enliven the game's main story. The quests in an role-playing game (RPG) like *Skyrim*, for instance, involve characters with stories and troubles that represent subplots scattered liberally throughout the game.

Finally, stories can keep players playing even when gameplay gets stale. There are a limited number of mechanics and unique areas that can be added to a game. Those assets are expensive, both in terms of developer time and memory requirements. There's always a risk of players getting

Courtesy of Pixabay, at https://pixabay.com/vectors/alice-in-wonderland-animals-tale-30130/.

bored after lopping off the head of the one-thousandth orc. But what might that orc have been guarding? What twist will players discover as they explore his lair? Adding story elements is much faster and cheaper (in development costs) than motivating players with new progression systems ("let's add fishing!") or rewards. An evolving story gives players a reason to keep plowing through all those orcs.

One thing to remember about game stories—in almost all big-budget games, story is secondary to gameplay. Story exists to support the gameplay experience the team wants players to receive. Every aspect of the story should work to enhance that experience. Players are in a game to enjoy *gameplay*, not read masses of text, listen to endless spiels from NPCs (nonplayer characters), or watch interminable cinematics.

As much as possible, put yourself in the player's shoes. Does the story you're adding support gameplay and motivate the player, or does it add friction at a time when the player wants to rush forward?

WHO CREATES A GAME'S STORY?

The game's story is the narrative designer's responsibility, but the project's creative director (CD) and game design lead usually determine the overall direction of the story, which needs to complement the intended gameplay experience. The actual story details are left to the narrative designer to flesh out, with the aid of other game designers and scripters who help implement it and add their own creative touches.

The CD may supply the overarching vision, but it's the narrative designer's job to transform that vision into concrete design documents and a written script. The narrative designer oversees the day-to-day efforts to bring the CD-approved story to life. Think of the narrative designer as the CD's point person in charge of story integrity.

PLOT VS. STORY

Many people use the words "plot" and "story" interchangeably, but they have very different meanings. Plot is the skeleton of the story, the series of events that unfolds from the game's start to its finish. Story is created from that plot when you add characters to the mix; how the plot's events affect the characters and how they react to those events are the truly compelling aspects of a story.

PLOT

STORY

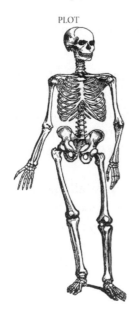

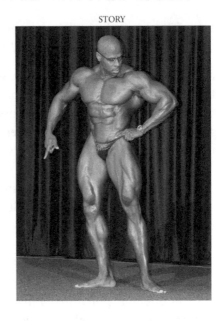

Courtesy of FreeSVG.org

Courtesy of Eric J. Cutright, Wikimedia Commons. https://commons.wikimedia.org/wiki/File:US_Navy_070504-N-0995C-072_Chief_Mineman_Kevin_Sperling_appears_as_the_guest_body_builder_at_an_Armed_Forces_body_building_competition_held_at_Sharkey%27s_Theatre_at_Naval_Station_Pearl_Harbor.jpg

People are fascinated by people. A dry recounting of a sequence of events leaves readers unmoved, no matter how important the events might be. But show readers the human impact of those events, and you have a story worth reading. Characters make a story. Designers often forget this, getting caught up in the excitement of building a world, mistaking history and events for a story that will engage players.

When I talk to my narrative design students about plot vs. story, I give them an assignment to help them see how an intriguing story can develop from a simple plot. This assignment (the "Arcade Game Short Story" assignment in the Narrative Design I class in Appendix C) asks students to choose an arcade game that currently has no real story and to write a short story about that game. The story needs to be set in the world depicted in the game and it needs to focus on a character in that game. Good choices for this assignment are games like *Frogger, Asteroids, Pac-Man, Space Invaders, Galaga, Dig-Dug,* and so on.

Courtesy of GoodFreePhotos.com.

These arcade games contain a simple plot (frog crosses road, spaceship pilot navigates an asteroid field, etc.). Students are asked to create a story from that plot. Those stories need to revolve around the characters in the arcade games. The stories need to tell the reader who those characters are, how they got into that situation, what they're doing there, and so on. They need to turn a sequence of events into an interesting story.

Students have come up with some great stories. Did you know, for example, that Pac-Man is a drug addict, running around the corridors of a psychiatric hospital, popping pills, and hallucinating he's being chased by ghosts? Or that Frogger is a college kid in a frog costume, drunkenly staggering home from a Halloween party? One student brought the world of Missile Command to life by setting it within the context of the Cuban Missile Crisis of 1962.

These kinds of adaptations happen all the time outside the classroom. Several of the games I've worked on have been game adaptations of someone else's IP (intellectual property). While I was still at TSR back in the mid-1980s, working on Dungeons & Dragons (D&D) and Advanced Dungeons & Dragons (AD&D) games, I also worked on a pen-and-paper Conan RPG and an Indiana Jones RPG; those were adaptations from books and movies, respectively. In the video game industry, I've worked on a *Jeopardy* game, a game based on the *Robin Hood: Prince of Thieves* movie, one based on the *Punisher* comic books, the *Carmen Sandiego* TV series, the *Top Gun* movie, and more.

Learning to take an existing IP and convert it into a game is a valuable skill for game designers and narrative designers. People who have never done this before often think of the existing IP as a straitjacket that limits a game's tone and setting. In my experience, it's actually very freeing. The IP gives you the basic setting, background story and characters, and a solid foundation for your game's story. This frees you to create a unique story for players set against a background they already know and love.

We work on game adaptations in my narrative classes, first with the arcade game short story assignment and later with a concept document assignment aimed at envisioning a game made from an IP that already exists in another medium. The instructions for both assignments, plus the template for the game adaptation concept doc, can be found in Appendix C.

TELLING STORIES WITHOUT WRITING

One of the key lessons narrative designers learn is how to tell stories without words. Visual storytelling in games is always a joint effort between narrative designers, artists, and level designers. Working together, you build an environment that tells the story to the player. When players work out what's happening (or learn what has already happened) by exploring the world around them, they engage more strongly with the story and world and feel like they're discovering these details rather than simply being talked at.

Imagine walking into a village. A resident runs up to you and immediately launches into a long, boring story about how a dragon attacked the village five years ago and they've been slowly rebuilding ever since.

Courtesy of Planet-Science.com.

That's how you force-feed a story to players. Now imagine that you walk into the same village and are greeted by the same person. This time, they walk you through the village, talking about some problem the village is currently suffering from. As you walk along, you notice a few toppled structures and faded scorch marks nearby. Ivy has grown up along the walls and partially covered up the damage. There are also newer buildings in town, all of them made of stone instead of wood. Without the villager saying a word about it, you've likely pieced together the story: A fire-breathing dragon attacked the village, but it happened long enough ago that plant growth has covered up some of the damage. Maybe later you can find someone to ask about this.

That's visual (or environmental) storytelling. It allows the player to piece together the story and leaves room for them to make up their own version of events. This gets the player more engaged with your game and its world.

Narrative designers also work with sound designers to tell stories via audio cues. Screams off in the distance or monstrous roars from unseen sources will get your players' minds racing with possibilities (and tension).

When I worked on the *Elder Scrolls Online*, most of my time on that project was spent in the PvP (player vs. player) province of Cyrodiil. I worked with the artists, level designers, and our Quality Assurance (QA) team to build visual storytelling into that vast landscape. I asked the rest of the team to search for areas that didn't have much going on and to think of interesting objects to add. In a cave along a stream I added three skel-etons, one of them clutching a note from their commander ordering them to spy on the enemy camp. A level designer added an excavated hole with an open casket at the bottom; I added a note from a nephew apologizing to his uncle's ghost for disturbing his rest and stealing a family heirloom. Our QA team sent in reports of dull areas; artists and level designers would take a look and add something interesting to it. Visual storytelling takes effort and coordination among different disciplines, but it's almost always worth it.

CHAPTER 4

Game Development as a Craft

G AME DESIGN IS A CRAFT. It's a set of skills that you learn by doing. And these are skills you learn best alongside those who've been doing it longer than you, as mentioned in Chapter 2.

The best college can do is prepare you to be an apprentice in the game industry; the classes you've taken can't simulate the real environment of a professional game development team. You're going to improve dramatically by working alongside masters of your trade, being on a team with folks who've been doing what you want to do for a long time. If you're not working alongside those who know a lot more about your chosen field, then you'll be making the same mistakes every new, untutored game developer makes in their first few years in the industry.

There's a definite apprentice → journeyman → master structure within every discipline in the game industry. Many companies recognize this and build it into their organizational structure. At some companies, a shiny new college graduate gets slotted into a junior designer position (or junior animator, coder, artist, etc.). After a few years, they get promoted to Designer. A few years more and they're bumped up to Senior Designer. And eventually they could move up to Lead Designer. A move up from there could be to creative director (though a CD can come from a variety of disciplines). Some game development companies have a Studio Designer position who oversees the designers on every project at the company. Other companies assign experience levels to all disciplines within a game development team. So you might start out as a Level 1 Designer and move up a rank every year or two, eventually peaking at Level 5.

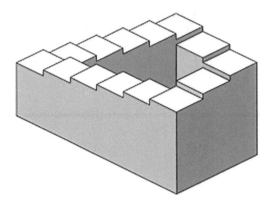

Courtesy of Wikipedia. https://en.wikipedia.org/wiki/Penrose_stairs.

Regardless of the system a particular company uses, there's a clear hierarchy at almost all game industry companies. This is an explicit recognition of the value that's added as employees accumulate years of experience in the industry. Mixing designers (and programmers, animators, artist, etc.) of various experience levels on a team sets up a mentoring system in which the tricks of the trade are passed along from the veterans down to the newbies (who rapidly become veterans and mentors themselves).

When someone is leaving or celebrating a work anniversary at a game company, many times they express how much they've learned from others while on the job. No matter how much you think you've learned in college—trust me, there's much more. And the best place to learn is in the industry, working with experienced colleagues.

Thinking that you can learn about game design and development by playing games is akin to believing you're ready for the National Basketball Association (NBA) because you've watched a lot of basketball games. LeBron James and I both watched lots of basketball games, but only one of us spent the thousands of hours actually playing the game needed to develop the skills necessary to make it in the NBA. I'll leave it to you to figure out which one of us that is.

Likewise, reading articles on Gamasutra or attending sessions at the Game Developers Conference doesn't grant you the design skills needed to break into the game industry. Those can help, but only a little. To develop the necessary skills, you need to actually design games. To really know what it takes to create AAA games, you need to experience life on a game development team, working alongside your teammates 8–10 hours a day for months and years at a time. That's how you learn. Everything that came before that, every class you took, every lecture you attended, every article you read—all that just helped you prepare for that intensive learning experience.

If you're an independent developer or working for a small indie company, you have an even steeper learning curve because it's all on you. Your skill development comes from your own efforts—your creativity and dedication in designing and iterating on your games. How well you learn from your successes and failures determines how rapidly your skills improve.

SOFT SKILLS

Most good game companies value experience highly when hiring. Often, their ideal candidate isn't a recent grad; it's an industry veteran who has learned the lessons that come from years of daily work on a game dev team. It's actually a warning sign when a company is more interested in hiring recent grads than veterans. That's an indication they are looking for newbies whose desperation to make it into the industry renders them easy targets for the predatory practices of overwork and underpay.

Experienced developers are expected to have "soft skills." That's the term for interpersonal skills such as negotiating to a compromise, solving problems collaboratively, and pitching in to help others when it's not really your job to do so. Some people are born with these skills, but most develop them from working alongside others for years. No one survives long in a collaborative environment like the game industry without learning these skills. They are what enable you to work with the same group of people for years without strangling any of them, no matter how much you may be tempted.

Courtesy of Cliparts101.com.

Some of us learn soft skills growing up (if, for example, you're the sixth in a family of nine kids). Others learn them working on group projects in secondary school. But others are never put in situations in which they have to learn soft skills; those people don't last long in the game industry.

In short: If you're a student, make it your goal to get as much practice collaborating with others as possible during your college years.

There are many ways for instructors to incorporate soft skills in game design and narrative design classes. In my classes at Webster University, every written assignment is followed up with either a small-group workshop (3–4 students per group) or peer reviews done online. In either case, students read each other's work and give constructive feedback. Students learn and practice the basic precepts of giving feedback—careful consideration of how well the work fits assignment requirements, the need to reinforce good work with positive feedback, and the art of providing helpful suggestions to improve substandard work.

I see noticeable improvement in the quality of feedback students give each other over the course of the semester. Students who practice these skills come into each successive class with better feedback skills each time.

Feedback drives the revision cycle that greatly contributes to the improvement of games, but it also contributes to the improvement of individual game developers. Giving and receiving feedback are two distinct and vital skills. Students need to practice giving feedback in a nonjudgmental way, so the recipient doesn't take offense and is willing to listen to suggestions. Students also learn to listen with an open mind to all suggestions, even ones that may not be couched in the most diplomatic terms. This is not easy to do! But it's essential. I've seen game developers fired for being unable to accept feedback on their work.

Collaboration is another vital soft skill for game developers. That's why all those who teach game industry disciplines should incorporate as much group work as possible into their classes. This differs from workshops and feedback. As a student team member, you're not critiquing others' work but instead working on a joint project that requires teammates to channel their creativity in directions that advance the project. For many students, this is a new experience. Learning to negotiate with others to come to a mutually agreed-upon game design, then working together to implement that concept, is a key experience for budding game developers. It's also one they'll wind up describing in interviews with prospective employers. Students should seek out classes that require collaboration.

Courtesy of Wikimedia Commons. https://commons.wikimedia.org/wiki/File:Curb_
Your_Ego_close_crop.jpg

In addition to keeping one's ego in check during development, being able to contribute to brainstorming sessions is a critical part of a developer's job. These can be formal meetings called to discuss an issue facing the team as a whole, or informal gatherings around someone's desk to discuss a small-scale problem. These sessions drive creativity and innovation across a game development team. Your ability to contribute to these efforts is a big part of your value to a game company. And that comes only with the experience that years of collaborative projects give you.

Collegiality is another soft skill vital to creative industries. You don't have to like everyone you work with (you almost certainly won't), but you do have to be able to work with them on the common goal of creating the best game you can. Being able to put aside prior clashes and pull together in the same direction is an important element of being a team player.

Any group activities—workshops, design tasks, feedback sessions, reviews—serve to strengthen students' collaboration skills. Students should be sure to point out these activities to prospective employers when trying to break into the industry. This can help ease employers' concerns about the ability of recent graduates to work well with others.

There's a lot of give-and-take on a team project, a lot of tamping down one's ego for the sake of the team and game. Most people tend to champion their own ideas, or their own department, over other work they're less connected to. The trick is to remember that it's the team's game you are working on, not your own. Argue for what's best for the player experience, even when it's difficult, inconvenient, or involves another developer's pet project.

Your hard skills, the skills within your chosen discipline, may get you into the game industry, but your soft skills determine how long you remain. The ability to work well with others, to subsume your ego to the needs of the team and project, is what makes an employee truly valuable.

CHAPTER 5

The Idea Is Everything... and Nothing

WHERE DO YOU GET YOUR IDEAS?

Game designers get asked this question all the time. (So do a lot of other creatives.) As far as I'm concerned, there's no great secret to it. The best game ideas come outside the medium of games. Ideas can come from art, literature, music, nature, film, news, and world events. They can come from dreams, overheard conversations, or something seen on a walk. Real life and everything in it can be a source of inspiration for game ideas.

Will Wright got the idea for *The Sims*, one of the best-selling games of all time, after he lost his home in a fire and had to buy new furniture and household goods. *Pokémon*'s co-creator Satoshi Tajiri was inspired by his childhood hobby of collecting insects. The inspiration for *Assassin's Creed* came from a Slovenian novel written in 1938. Good ideas can come from anywhere!

Sometimes designers get their ideas from other games, especially innovative game systems and game mechanics to use in their games. There are certainly successful games that meld mechanics from different genres. The mobile game *10,000,000*, for example, is a match-3 game at heart, but it includes strong role-playing game (RPG) and endless runner aspects, merging those three very different game genres into an enjoyable experience. In a similar fashion, *Empires & Puzzles* merges match-3 game mechanics with RPG mechanics and strong social elements to create an engaging and addictive game. There are lots of examples of games borrowing mechanics from other games.

But designers often get their best ideas from thinking outside the game box. Get off your chair and head out into the world. Walk along a busy street, absorbing all the activity around you. Put yourself in different places, see new things, and have novel experiences. Go sit in a coffee shop, restaurant, or museum to people-watch and listen to conversations. People are telling each other stories all the time; a bit of eavesdropping can give you a great idea for a new game. Take notes on anything interesting you see or hear. Watch the news for stories about people and events.

New experiences that can trigger game ideas don't have to involve listening to or watching people. Go to a library, walk along the shelves, and look at book titles. Read a book that is outside your usual genre. Get into a park or nature trail and take a walk, watching and listening to the world around you. You're not going to have innovative ideas when you're stuck in the same rut all the time. Change things up on yourself; get away from games and game design. If all you do with your life is play games, you're limiting your ability to innovate. Go out and look for stories to inspire you.

Here's an example from my own career. A few years ago, I was asked to interview for a game designer position at a small company. They wanted me to present a couple of game ideas as part of the interview process. Just before this, I had finished reading a book called *Abundance* by Sena Jeter Naslund.[1] It was an historical novel about Marie Antoinette. When I got the call to come up with game concepts, I instantly thought of one set during the French Revolution. I wrote up a concept and brief Game Design Document (GDD) and created a presentation for the company based on those documents. I never would have come up with the game idea if I hadn't just read that novel.

THE POWER OF YOUR SUBCONSCIOUS

Getting out and exploring the world will engage your subconscious mind in your creative activities. Your subconscious is an incredible source of great ideas, but you have to give it something to work with. Experiencing the same things day after day isn't going to do it. New experiences, different sights, and unusual sounds—those activate the creative potential of your subconscious.

Your subconscious can also be a wellspring of solutions for problems you encounter in your work. When you're in the game industry, you may work on a project for months, often years, at a time. You're always thinking about it. Any problems or roadblocks you encounter, your subconscious is working on

---

[1] Naslund, S. J. (2006). *Abundance: A novel of Marie Antoinette*, William Morrow: New York City.

them overtime all day and night long. You'll often wake up with something new to try, a potential solution suggested by your hardworking subconscious.

For students, the situation is different. You're juggling lots of very different tasks and activities every day. You might have five or six classes per semester, a social life, a full-time or part-time job, family obligations, and more. A particular class assignment doesn't usually get thought about much, on a day-to-day basis, amid everything else that's going on. And that hampers the creativity you can bring to the task, as you are not engaging your subconscious to help you out.

My advice is to try hard not to leave assignments until the last minute. As soon as an assignment is available, spend a few minutes reading it, thinking about it, and jotting down a few notes. That gets your subconscious involved that night while you sleep (or work on mundane tasks). When you wake up, new ideas may very well have cropped up overnight. Jot them down; take a few minutes the next day to add more ideas to your notes and to expand upon your previous thoughts.

Doing a little bit of work each day on an assignment engages your subconscious and brings more creativity to the task. You'll end up spending the same amount of time (or less!) working daily as if you waited until the last minute and crammed something together to submit just before the deadline. But your work is likely to end up much more imaginative and creative, and you'll garner a better grade as well.

Students who engage the power of their subconscious have told me this has helped them overcome writer's and designer's block at crucial times.

A book called *The Defence of Duffer's Drift*[2] brings this lesson home. It's probably the world's most entertaining military training manual, but it has two strong lessons for game design, which is why I like to share it with students.

I was introduced to this book over 30 years ago by some colleagues who played wargames with me at TSR. The book was written in 1904 by Captain E.D. Swinton of the British Army. Its intent is to teach infantry officers in training about small-unit tactics in wartime. It has been used by military academies all over the world for over 115 years. Captain Swinton later became Major General Swinton and is credited with the invention of the tank prior to World War I. This is a guy who thought outside the box.

Duffer's Drift follows the misadventures of young Lieutenant Backsight Forethought, newly commissioned and given his first command, during the Boer War in 1899–1902. Lt. Forethought is given 50 men and told to

---

[2] Swinton, E.D. (1904), *The Defence of Duffer's Drift*, W. Clowes & Sons: London.

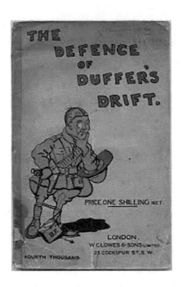

Courtesy of Wikimedia Commons. https://commons.wikimedia.org/wiki/
File:The_Defence_of_Duffer%27s_Drift_cover.jpg

defend Duffer's Drift, a strategic ford across a river. A large contingent of
Boer fighters is expected to try to cross there and the lieutenant is ordered
to prevent this at all costs.

Lt. Forethought and his men arrive at the drift and set up camp.
That night, he has a nightmare about the Boers attacking and wiping out
his ill-prepared command. He awakens the next morning and goes about
rectifying all the gaps in his defenses that his dream revealed to him. Then
he goes to sleep again that night and has another dream. Again his command is overwhelmed, but his fixes help them make a better showing.
Problems still exist, and the next morning Forethought starts rectifying
them. Sentries are repositioned, trenches are dug, spies are rounded up,
and so on.

This goes on for several nights. Forethought's dreams point out smaller
and smaller problems each time, and his command does better with every
successive imaginary battle. Finally, when the Boer forces eventually
arrive and launch a real attack, Lt. Forethought's troops hold the ford and
repulse the attack.

This book illustrates two lessons that are critical for game designers
or anyone involved in creative work. The first is to engage the problem-
solving ability of your subconscious. Give your brain something to chew
on while you sleep and you'll often have great ideas when you awaken.
Many authors rely on the power of their dreams: Stephen King has said

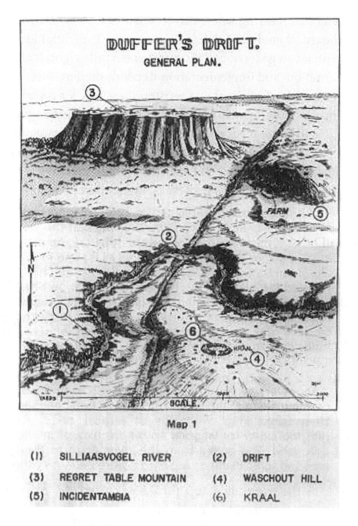

Courtesy of RegimentalRogue.com.

in interviews that a nightmare he had on a plane gave him the story for *Misery*, which became one of his most acclaimed books. You may even want to keep a dream journal to record these fleeting inspirations.

The second lesson for game design is the value of iteration—the playtesting and revision cycle. Iteration isn't a chore; it's the key to creating great games. Generally, the more times a game goes through the iteration cycle of create-playtest-feedback-revision, the more fun and seamless it will be. The greatest game idea in the world will produce a terrible game without enough iteration. An unimaginative game idea can result in a great game with enough iteration. (The inspiration for the movie *Aliens* came from a pitch meeting where director James Cameron wrote "Alien" on a chalkboard, then drew a dollar sign after it.) The initial idea is just a starting point; it can go terribly wrong or wonderfully right. It all depends on implementation, and implementation depends on iteration.

The Defence of Duffer's Drift was written long ago, for a very different audience and purpose, but it has valuable lessons for game designers today. Find the book, give it a read, and it will illustrate these two vital lessons. If you teach game design or narrative design, I recommend discussing the book in your classes, to bring home the importance of both one's subconscious and of iteration in the game development process.

IDEAS AND GAMES

The idea for a game is a tiny fraction of the work needed to create a finished product. Much more creativity and effort go into all the subsequent stages of game development. Coming up with an idea is the easy part.

Thomas Edison is credited with saying, "Genius is one percent inspiration and ninety-nine percent perspiration." He meant that the initial ideas were just a tiny part of the process of creating a new device or other invention. He knew what he was talking about: His methodical testing methods and large teams of scientists created the foundation of modern R&D.

For work in the game industry, think of game design as one percent inspiration and ninety-nine percent implementation. Coming up with an idea for a game is far and away the easiest part of the process, and that initial concept makes up far less than one percent of the work to be done in creating that game.

Courtesy of Wikimedia Commons. https://commons.wikimedia.org/wiki/File:Thomas_Edison2-crop.jpg

Another way to think of this is in terms of value. An idea for a game has almost no value. It's not that difficult to come up with 50 game ideas in a week. They're cheap, easy, and mostly worthless. Much of the creative effort for a game occurs after the initial idea is proposed. All the work that goes into making a game is what gives a game its value, not the initial idea. Think of it this way, in terms of increasing value:

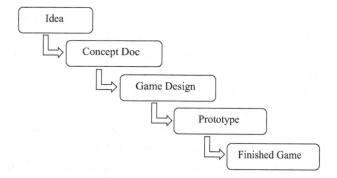

This is why game companies aren't really interested in stealing anyone else's ideas. Not only is the initial idea just a tiny fraction of the work needed to create a game, but anyone at a game company can supply many concepts for games. All of the ideas current employees come up with are likely to be more appropriate for that company, as they are vastly more familiar with the skillsets present within the company, the internal tools they have to work with, the audience that buys their games, and their usual budgets. Their game ideas are likely to play to those strengths.

CONCEPT DOCUMENTS

Turning a game idea into a brief concept document gives it some value. You've thought about the idea enough to formalize elements of it (such as story, setting, gameplay, and so on) into a short document. This process forces you to consider how the game would actually work, which winnows out obviously unworkable ideas. A concept doc can be presented to management as a proposal to be considered for further development. (See the next section for more discussion about concept docs, along with a template for creating them.)

If you are a student, be sure to write up multiple concept documents. This book includes three templates for concepts—one on the following page and the other two in Appendix C. The template here is for an entertainment game; the two in Appendix C are for a serious/educational game and for a game adaptation, respectively. Create a one-page concept to fit each template. Sticking to a single page forces you to concentrate on the most critical elements of your design, stripping away wordiness and lack of focus. In a narrative design class, you could choose one of these docs upon which to build the work that you create for the remainder of the semester.

Think of your concept documents as cheat sheets (or summary sheets, if you prefer) that you can hand out to the audience when you're presenting your game idea. The audience consists of company execs, managers, and people who don't want to read a lot to get the gist of what you're saying. So keep it simple, direct, and focused. The concept doc contains the basic, high-level information, while the presentation supplies more detail. And the concept doc serves to remind your audience of the highlights of your idea long after the presentation is over.

Note that in the templates, the italicized text are instructions to help supply the information needed in the concept doc.

Most of the games I've worked on in my career have fallen into the entertainment category. These started with a concept document, as outlined above. For these games, the player's enjoyment is paramount and the concept and GDDs (which are much longer and more involved than the initial concept doc) that follow focus on that. Ensuring that the game engages players, entertains them, and challenges them is an ongoing consideration throughout this type of game's development.

I've also worked on a number of educational or serious-minded games. Those started with the second type of concept doc and proceeded from there into the GDD phase. In these games, the player needs to stand a decent chance of learning something. This means that delivering informative content competes with the usual goal of creating something your audience will enjoy. Games that teach players about global warming, famine, diabetes, dementia, and so on are valuable additions to the medium of games and society at large. But these games also need to engage players and provide interesting challenges and/or story to maintain players' attention.

The third type of concept doc is for game adaptations. Throughout my career, I've had many opportunities to work on intellectual property (IP) created in one medium that a team then adapts into a game. While at TSR, in addition to working on D&D and AD&D game products, I also worked on RPGs based on the Indiana Jones movies and the Conan books (by Robert E. Howard). Once I moved into the digital game realm, I worked on many game adaptations, from games based on the *Punisher* series of graphic novels to those based on movies like *Top Gun, Robin Hood: Prince of Thieves,* and *Home Alone 2.* The work I did on the *Elder Scrolls Online* Massively Multiplayer Online (MMO) could be considered an adaptation of a single-player game into a massively multiplayer setting. At this writing, I am working on a board game based on the fantasy novel *God's Demon,* by Wayne Barlow, my latest IP-based project.

As you can see, game developers can expect to have opportunities to work on adaptations of IP from other industries. The assignment for

CONCEPT DOCUMENT TEMPLATE—ENTERTAINMENT GAME

GAME TITLE:

Give your game a name! Leave this until after you've filled out the rest of the template.

INTENDED AUDIENCE:

Who is your game intended for? Who will enjoy it?

HIGH CONCEPT:

Describe your game in just a few sentences.

GENRE:

What type of game is it? What sorts of games is it similar to?

DESCRIPTION:

Describe the look and feel of your game. Briefly describe the game world, the player's place in it, and so on. Give more detail than in the "High Concept" section above.

STORY:

What is your game's story? Why is the player here and what is s/he doing? What is his/her eventual goal? (Even if your game doesn't have an explicit story, with characters and dialogue, it should have background and goal(s) for the player.)

SETTINGS/ENVIRONMENTS:

List and briefly detail the setting(s)/environment(s) in which your game takes place. What will the player see in your game? Where will s/he go?

FEATURES/GAMEPLAY:

List the important features of your game and give examples of its gameplay. This section should complement the "Description" section above, not duplicate it. A bullet list would work well. How does this gameplay fit your story and setting?

USPS:

What are your game's Unique Selling Points? What's different about it?

students to write a game adaptation concept document exposes them to this aspect of game development. Students can choose any IP they wish, as long as it hasn't already had a game adaptation created for it. Giving students this choice helps ensure that their topic is one that interests them, which makes for a more engaging experience.

One side note about creating a game based on an existing IP: Until you've actually done it, you might assume that it restricts and stifles your creativity. I've found it to be just the opposite. Having that pre-existing foundation upon which to build, thinking about what fans loved about that IP and resolving to build that experience into your game, gives you a solid direction to begin with, and enables you to be creative within a well-established framework. This can be a relief from the experience of staring at a blank canvas, puzzling out how to begin your game design, where to set it, and even what sort of game will be.

At one video game company where I worked, we had a project canceled and company management decided to have the team (minus the writer) work on just art, animation, sound, and coding, with no story foundation upon which to build. That team of roughly 40 experienced game developers floundered for over a month, unable to accomplish anything of note, until management finally came to its senses and ended the experiment. A solid foundation is critical to good design—sometimes, getting such a foundation in the form of established IP can be a massive boon.

In the game industry, once a concept is greenlit by management for further development, the next step is often for the team to create a GDD. This task usually falls to either the narrative designer, creative director, or lead designer. No matter who writes the initial version of the document, all the discipline leads review and comment on the GDD, taking it through multiple revisions. Management reviews these more-detailed plans for the game and either greenlights it to move into development or asks for further revisions and refinement (or sometimes cancels the project).

I like to simulate this stage of game development in game design and narrative design classes. Students choose one of the concept documents they wrote and develop that idea further within the context of a GDD. See the GDD templates in Appendix C; there's one for digital game designs, one for analog game designs (board, pen-and-paper RPG, card, etc.), and one for interactive fiction game designs. Moving from the concept stage to the GDD stage moves us firmly into pre-production. This and later stages of game development will be discussed in Chapter 9.

CHAPTER 6

The Player's the Thing

NOTHING ABOUT A GAME is as important as your audience: the player. You have to know your audience to understand the experience they're looking for. And if your game doesn't deliver that experience, it's headed right for the discount bin.

But what do players want? How do you decide what to include in your game and what to leave out? What's going to make players pick your game among the thousands they can choose from, play it, and keep playing it?

This is a question that has bedeviled hordes of developers. In this chapter, we'll learn how to answer it, step by step.

WHO ARE YOUR PLAYERS?

One way to learn about players is to analyze yourself as a gamer. Two well-known tools for this analysis are Bartle's Taxonomy and the Quantic Foundry (QF) survey.

Bartle's Taxonomy: A taxonomy is just a way to organize information into categories or into a hierarchy. In the mid-1990s, Richard Bartle published a paper[1] that categorized players according to their actions or motivations within a game. He divided players into four basic groups—Achievers, Explorers, Killers, and Socializers.

---

[1] Bartle, R., *Hearts, Clubs, Diamonds, Spades: Players Who Suit MUDs*, 1996, published at http://mud.co.uk/richard/hcds.htm.

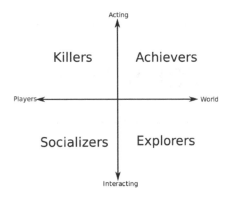

Courtesy of Wikipedia. https://en.wikipedia.org/wiki/Bartle_taxonomy_of_player_
types

Achievers strive to conquer the world and everything in it. They want to be at the top of leaderboards, complete every quest, find every item, and so on. They want to act upon the world and beat the game.

Explorers are motivated to poke their way into every nook and cranny of a game world, to find every hidden area, and to uncover every secret. They take joy in discovery, on interacting with the world.

Killers are an odd group; their desire is to act on other players. Some Killers like to ruin others' gameplay experiences, by griefing, team-killing, and other acts of malicious mayhem. Other Killers try to help others, to improve their experiences in the game. Imagine you're a new character in a game, venturing into the wilderness clad in only Level 1 rags and clutching a sharp stick. Suddenly, a glowing paladin on a Pegasus flies down, drops a load of fancy weapons and sturdy armor at your feet and then flies off. That player is a Killer too, but one who acts on other players in a positive way.

Finally, *Socializers* play to interact with other people. They're the folks who spend all their game time in guilds, accompanying others on raids, and crafting items to help other players. In a single-player game, Socializers will get satisfaction from talking to interesting non-player characters (NPCs) and learning their stories.

Though we often talk about these motivations as if they were separate player archetypes, in reality you'll find a mix of all of these impulses in most players. No one is 100% Achiever or Explorer or Killer or Socializer. That mix depends not only on the game we're playing but also the mood we're in during that play session. In a first-person shooter, I might be 50% Achiever, 25% Killer, and 25% Explorer. If I'm in a bad mood, I might be more Killer than Explorer. In a role-playing game (RPG), I might be 30% Explorer, 30% Achiever, 25% Socializer, and 15% Killer.

When playing an analog (tabletop) game, such as a board game, card game, or pen-and-paper role-playing game, there's always a Socializer motivation. By definition, tabletop games are social rituals that bring friends together around a table. Where the other motivations come in depends greatly on the type of game you're playing and who you're playing it with.

Bartle's Taxonomy is a highly useful tool for profiling your players, but it's also flexible and open to interpretation. Keep this in mind, and don't forget that it changes depending on the type of game being played.

Quantic Foundry: This group gathers information about gamers and their gaming motivations via an online survey on their website (https://quanticfoundry.com). The survey builds a profile by asking questions about what sorts of games you play and why you play them. It builds a profile of you as a game player. This profile is more detailed than Bartle's classifications, but it doesn't consider that you play different games for different reasons.

Here is a two-fold assignment that will lend insight into player motivation (see the "Self as Player" assignment in Appendix C). The first part asks you to consider several genres of games that you play and think about what motivates you to play that type of game. You assign percentages to all four Bartle motivations (adding up to 100%) for each of those genres. Then explain the reasoning behind your breakdown.

The second half of the assignment is to go to the QF site and take the gamer survey on it. For digital gamers, this survey is on the QF home page, with a link to get your Gamer Motivation Profile. For analog gamers, clicking on the Lab link in the upper right of the QF home page brings up a page whose first paragraph contains a link to their Board Game Motivations Profile.

Taking the survey generates graphs that depict your primary and secondary gaming motivations. The graphs look like spider webs, if the spider had been dosed with lysergic acid diethylamide (LSD). However, they make it easy to visualize the balance between your motivations as a player.

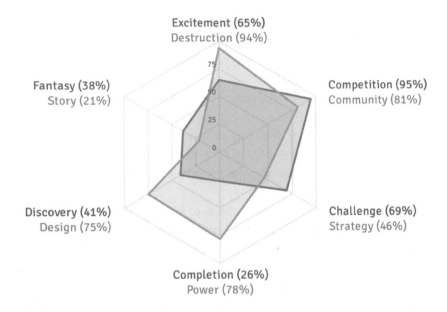

Excitement (65%)
Destruction (94%)

Fantasy (38%)
Story (21%)

Competition (95%)
Community (81%)

75
50
25
0

Discovery (41%)
Design (75%)

Challenge (69%)
Strategy (46%)

Completion (26%)
Power (78%)

Courtesy of Quantic Foundry.

Now compare the two side-by-side: the breakdown of your motivations according to Bartle's Taxonomy, and the graphs from the QF survey. Which one do you feel most accurately captured the reasons you play games?

If this assignment is completed in a classroom or game design group, review at least two others' self-analyses. Usually, you'll find an incredible variation in player motivations.

Here's the point: Only a small fraction of the audience for your games thinks just like you. The audience you're targeting is far more diverse than you might think. It's essential to consider the potential breadth of your audience as you decide on the gameplay, story, and aesthetics of your game.

WHAT DO PLAYERS WANT?

Here's a similar exercise. List as many game genres as you can, then write down the one or two core game mechanics in each. What are the keys to creating the player experience? When instructors go through this exercise with a classroom of students, they necessarily consider only successes, games that delivered experiences players loved; the games that didn't are quickly forgotten.

What do players want from an FPS or TPS (first-person or third-person shooter)? How about a MOBA (multiplayer online battle arena, such as *League of Legends*)? Or an RPG? To get a different perspective on those questions, the class can create a list of genres. Students should agree on the one or two game mechanics that are most critical to delivering the experience players want. This exercise can help students think more about where the efforts of developers (including themselves!) should be concentrated when creating games in any genre.

For example, considering the FPS/TPS genre, the class might decide the most important elements are great combat mechanics and a wide variety of weapons and equipment. By isolating these mechanics, we've found the areas where developers should focus their efforts—the mechanics that deliver the most bang for the buck.

HOW ARE YOU GOING TO DELIVER THAT EXPERIENCE?

You've now picked a genre and considered that genre's audience. Next, you need a plan of attack for actually implementing everything your players want—and surprising them with things they didn't know they wanted.

Your game's mechanics—the nuts and bolts of how it actually works—need to be strong. Be critical, even brutal, in your evaluations of them. Players certainly will be.

Ask how each mechanic improves the player experience. When you can't come up with a good answer, it's time to leave that concept on the cutting room floor. As Strunk and White admonish in their classic textbook[2] on writing, "Omit needless words!" Interrogate your mechanics just as rigorously, then polish the hell out of everything that makes the cut.

This isn't a one-time exercise, either. Examine your game and its mechanics at multiple points throughout development. As we discussed earlier, games change and evolve every day; mechanics need to change as well to stay in sync. If an idea that made sense in the initial concept no longer works six months into development, don't hesitate to cut. Your concern isn't to preserve your own work, but to deliver a coherent and engaging final product.

PLAYTESTING

There's no need to guess at what players want from your game. As early as possible, and as often as feasible, get others' thoughts on your design

---

[2] Strunk, W. Jr., & White, E. B. (1969). *The Elements of Style*, Macmillan: New York City.

plans during pre-production. Show your game design plans to students, instructors, game developers, and game players—anyone who's willing to read through them and give you feedback. Even if it's hard to ask for (and receive), this feedback could be the difference between success and failure. The earlier someone points out problems with your plans, the cheaper, faster, and easier it is to fix those issues. Discovering a fundamental problem with your design later, when you're deep into production, can cost your team thousands of hours of effort.

Likewise, playtest often during production, once you have gameplay for players to give feedback on. It doesn't matter how rough or incomplete your game is: Get it in front of testers and get their suggestions. You can guide their feedback into useful channels by telling them beforehand what you know is incomplete or broken and by asking for feedback on specific aspects of the game. This helps testers deliver feedback that's most useful to you.

One important thing to remember about playtesting feedback is that you don't have to do everything everyone says. Some of the feedback you get will be contradictory. You are the creator of this work and you need to determine which feedback helps improve your game and which doesn't. Just be sure to set aside your ego and consider each piece of advice solely in the light of whether it helps improve your game.

Keep in mind that you're not fully representative of the audience for your game, but everyone you invite to playtest it represents a slice of that audience. Their feedback can be surprising and upsetting, but put your ego aside and listen to every suggestion and comment. This is a direct response from your intended audience: It's the best way to tell if you're hitting the mark or not.

REMEMBER, THE PLAYER'S THE THING

It all comes back to the player. To have the best shot at delivering a successful game, you need to know your players, know what they want from your game, and focus your efforts on the elements that are critical to delivering that experience (and more!). It's a plus to surprise players with a new mechanic, or a twist on an old one; but that new addition must always meaningfully enhance the player experience. Don't add a mechanic just because it's unique, or because it seems cool. Keep your focus on the player and let the experience you're creating for them be your guide.

CHAPTER 7

The Team's the
Thing, Too

W E'VE TALKED ABOUT THE PLAYER, the audience for whom a game
is created, but what about the people who are going to make that
game? Different game genres require different skillsets to develop. Game
teams will always include diverse personalities, varying backgrounds, and
different outlooks on the place of games in our society. But one common
element to all successful teams is a melding of creativity from each team
member, all aimed at producing the best game possible. Teams that don't
coalesce into a common purpose generally fail to deliver a good game or
any game at all.

Beyond the need for a game development team to all pull in the same
direction, the aggregate of all the skillsets of team members needs to fit the
game to be created. The type and genre of game determine the skills that
are needed to create it, and the team composition flows from that.

In Chapter 4, we discussed the importance of soft skills to the success
of a game project and to the careers of all who work in the game industry.
The aggregate soft skills of the entire team often determine the success or
failure of the project.

The skillsets needed to create analog games (board games, card
games, pen-and-paper role-playing games (RPGs)) are a subset of those
required for digital (video and computer) games, so let's talk about the
latter teams first.

THE GAME DEVELOPMENT TEAM

For digital game projects, a wide range of disciplines and experience levels are needed to staff a team. On a large team, there will be multiple people in many of these roles. These teams usually have a lead for each discipline (design, narrative, sound, art, animation, and so on) who interacts with the other discipline leads. This person also leads those in their subteam, parceling out the tasks assigned to that discipline and keeping an eye on the pipeline for tasks moving through their area. On small teams, many folks will wear more than one hat, fulfilling multiple roles on the team.

Here's a brief rundown of the positions found on a digital game team.

Creative director (CD): This person oversees the creative efforts of everyone on the team. They are ultimately responsible for every design decision made during the project's development. This is much more of a management position than a day-to-day creative position, so it may not be a role that feels comfortable for hands-on developers who like to be involved in content creation from start to finish.

Producer: This person is in charge of scheduling, personnel issues, and interactions with company management. The producer position is parallel to that of the CD, with very distinct realms of responsibility. On a well-run team, the producer leaves all creative decisions to the CD, while the CD leaves all personnel and scheduling issues to the producer. On teams of more than 25 or so, you'll often find assistant/associate producers (ideally not too many, as a successful game dev team needs a lot more workers than managers).

Game designers: In all but the smallest companies, this group consists of several people (on large projects, dozens of folks fall in this category). These are the people who work out the game's systems, mechanics, and the challenges that players will face. This discipline should always have someone in the lead position (lead designer), reporting to the CD and guiding the other designers.

Other design disciplines (narrative, sound, level, scripting) often fall under the general umbrella of game design. Here are brief descriptions of these sub-disciplines:

Narrative designers perform the writing tasks required for the project. This includes non-player character (NPC) dialogue, equipment descriptions, and text that appear in-game. These designers often write many of the pre-production documents (concept docs, Game Design Docs, and so on) that are needed to ensure the entire team is on the same solid foundation when the implementation phase of the project begins. A narrative designer is often tasked with keeping the design documents updated as the game design changes (which it does on an almost daily basis).

Level designers (LDs) build the game's environments. These developers need both artistic and architectural skills to succeed at their job. After a level or region of a game is planned out (in a level design doc, zone design doc, or other document), LDs are usually the first ones to work on that area. They build the terrain in the game's engine and add in buildings (usually created by artists), trees and plants, and props, all of which add life to the setting. As LDs build environments, especially artificial ones, they ask what each space was created for, how it functions, and how its inhabitants use it.

LDs often complete their work in several passes. After laying out the terrain and buildings, an area is generally handed off to game designers or scripters who add in characters and events, fleshing the area out to test gameplay. Sometimes LDs need to come back to adjust the layout of the area to better accommodate the desired gameplay experience. After the gameplay pass, LDs return to layer in the area's flora and props in a final art pass.

Scripters are responsible for adding the gameplay to the area an LD has created. They use the game editor to add in NPCs for the player to interact with, giving these characters movement and actions, dialogue to speak to each other or the player character (PC), and reactions to the PC's presence in the game world. Scripters also add events that occur in the world around the PC, either triggered by the PC's actions or scheduled to occur at certain times, regardless of what the PC is doing.

Note that while level design and scripting are specific tasks with distinct skillsets, at some companies the same person will undertake both jobs. Those developers need to combine the artistic skills of level design with the game design sense needed for scripting.

Sound designers determine the aural landscape of the game, creating and implementing sound effects, ambient sounds, and music. These developers often create their own audio effects in their sound booths, but there are also libraries of stock sound effects that many sound designers use to save time. One of the operating principles of sound design is that every action the player undertakes should cause a sound to be heard. Walking along a corridor, opening a door, hitting something (or someone) with a weapon, suffering damage—all those activities should trigger a sound. The game world comes to life when the player notices it reacting to their every action.

Composers fall within the purview of the sound department, but their tasks and skillsets are often separate from those of sound designers. These developers create the musical score, which heightens the story's emotional impact. Sometimes a sound designer will also compose the music for a game, but many times these tasks are contracted out to a freelancer who specializes in video game scores.

Artists: Artists are responsible for the visual quality of the game. On smaller teams, the same one or two artists tackle a swath of art tasks, but in large teams, the department may be divided into many different titles and groups.

Concept artists create two-dimensional images of characters, items, and settings to provide a starting point for development. These are often based on text descriptions written by designers or discipline leads. These images bring the team's ideas for characters and places to life and give everyone a visual to agree upon (or debate) as the basis for implementation within the game.

Character artists work from concept art to create 2D sprites or 3D models (depending on the sort of game you're creating) of people, animals, and monsters that animators will bring to life by giving movement, facial expression, and gestures.

Vehicle and equipment artists create the sprites or 3D models of objects the PC can interact with in the game. These objects might be vehicles, weapons, armor, equipment, tools, books, and so on. These are objects that will be placed in the game world for the PC to interact with and to make the world feel more realistic.

Environment artists design objects that LDs use to bring the game world to life. They create buildings, plants, terrain features, clutter, and props—anything the LDs can add to make the world look more packed with detail and life. LDs and game designers interact often with environment artists, asking for new objects, requesting changes to existing ones, and collaborating to make areas of the game as interesting and engaging as possible.

User interface (UI) artists make the game's UI as appealing and intuitive as possible. All but the smallest game dev team will have an artist devoted to crafting the UI, along with a programmer whose job at least partly involves supporting that effort. The UI is the player's window into a digital world. It's vital to make the UI clean and intuitive, presenting the player with only the information they need in any situation.

Tech artists are a relatively new position, occupying a space in between artists and programmers. Tech artists help develop the tools artists need to undertake their tasks on a project, supplementing the game dev environment with add-ons to ease workflow and pipelines. These artists are more technically minded than most and form a necessary link between coders and artists.

Animation: This category includes two positions—animators and riggers. These used to be just two separate tasks lumped under animation, but as games have gotten more complex, two distinct sets of tasks emerged.

Riggers are the first to work on a model once the character artists are done with it. (They also work on vehicles, weapons, and other objects that have moving parts.) Riggers essentially put bones and joints inside a character model to enable parts to bend and move. Bones aren't just in the places real people (and creatures) have bones. If a character's hair is supposed to move when they run or the wind blows, that hair needs bones. If a character has a cape, that piece of clothing needs bones to enable it to flow naturally as the character moves. A horse's mane and tail need bones to look natural as the horse gallops along. For a character to have realistic facial expressions, there need to be bones placed around their mouth, cheeks, eyes, and eyebrows.

Animators work on the bone structure the riggers placed inside a model, determining the directions of movement, how far each bone moves, and synchronizing those movements among all the bones in a model. If you watch someone run, the animator needs to mimic all that synchronized movement in a running character—how the legs move in relation to each other, how the arms move, the hips, spine, head, etc. Given our innate awareness of how people and creatures really move, the animator (and rigger) have exacting jobs to do to make game characters seem to move realistically.

Coders: Programmers are the bedrock of any digital game development team. Everything that happens in a digital game depends on code. The amount of code written in-house depends on the decision to develop a unique game engine or not. Rolling your own engine puts a lot of burden on the shoulders of coders (and, usually, significantly extends the game's development time) but it gives you a lot of flexibility in finetuning the game engine to your team's exact needs. Using a third-party game engine, such as Unity or Unreal, makes for a much shorter development cycle at the expense of some flexibility and customization. Either way, everything in the game depends on its foundation of code, and the team's programmers are crucial to the implementation of all desired game mechanics. Technical limitations can often move these mechanics away from the forms designers originally envisioned.

Quality Assurance (QA): These are the developers who find all the holes and bugs in a game. Players will always try things developers don't expect. It's the testers in the QA department who push the limits of the game world and find all the unexpected edge cases. They find places where the game breaks down or works in odd ways, then they report the bug to the appropriate lead, who decides how (and if) someone should fix the problem.

While playing games all day sounds like a great job, it's not as much fun as you might think. If one tester falls through a crack in the world and an LD notes the issue as fixed, someone in the QA department needs to return to that location and possibly spend the next eight hours jumping and running all over the ground geometry to make sure the issue was really fixed. You can imagine how tedious this sometimes gets.

Courtesy of Needpix.com.

WORKING WITH EVERYONE

There are many moving parts and personalities that go into a game development team. It's not critical that you get along with everyone on your team, but it is crucial that you're able to work with them all.

There are some game dev disciplines that only need to interact with a few people most of the time. An animator, for example, might generally need to interact only with a rigger or two, a character artist, and the animation team lead. Occasionally they might go talk with a game designer or a programmer on a specific issue.

But other disciplines, especially the two we are most concerned with in this book, need to deal with many different folks every day. A narrative designer has writing and design duties that cause them to interact with people in every discipline, as the game's story affects every aspect of development. A game designer's duties might be limited to a certain section of the game, but those tasks could involve interacting with any member of the team, from coders to artists.

Regardless of one's official set of responsibilities, brainstorming, giving (and receiving) feedback, and adding creativity are always part of the job. When a team or part of a team is facing a problem, a brainstorming session is often the best way to come up with creative solutions. Gathering developers together from different disciplines provides a variety of ideas on how to fix the problem. When you're on a team, it's part of your job to accept the call to brainstorm and contribute to the group discussion.

As discussed in Chapter 4, feedback is a powerful engine for improving any game. Reviewing your teammates' work and giving them constructive feedback is an important aspect of your job. This is a skill that everyone should develop, ideally in school. The flip side of this is being able to take feedback. Every creative task involves at least some ego. Keeping yours in check when listening to others' feedback helps you accept different viewpoints on your work and gives you the opportunity to improve it. In game development, everyone represents some segment of your target audience, so listen to those opinions!

Remember that it's not your game, it's the team's game. Putting your ego aside gives you the best chance of maximizing your contribution to the project.

ANALOG GAME DEVELOPMENT TEAMS

The preceding paragraphs deal primarily with digital game development teams. Analog games (board games, card games, tabletop RPGs, etc.) have a much more streamlined team structure.

Analog game teams don't include coders, animators/riggers, sound designers/composers, LDs, and so on. They also generally don't have a CD; the lead designer usually fills that role. The remaining roles (game designers, artists, etc.) still exist, but there are far fewer people in those positions. Some of the digital game teams I've been on have had 30+ game designers, but the largest analog game team I was a part of had three game designers. Most analog games have a single artist who creates concept art, card art, game board art, and so on. Games that have many cards or other art needs (such as *Magic: The Gathering*) have a large stable of artists, in-house and freelance, who create the many images needed.

One position often found on analog projects but not on digital ones, is that of graphic artist. These folks are responsible for creating maps, tables, player aid cards, and so on.

At its most basic, an analog game needs only a few developers (or even a single developer with a variety of skillsets). A game designer and an artist could form a complete team for a board game. A tabletop RPG may need a couple of designers, a writer (or a designer with writing skills), and one or more artists. AAA analog teams can grow much larger, but nowhere near as large or varied as an AAA digital game.

WHAT THIS MEANS FOR INSTRUCTORS AND STUDENTS

So, how does all the above information affect students and their instructors? Look back at all the people who are on game development teams. On a big digital project (I've been on teams of up to 450 developers), there are dozens of folks in each of those positions. Think about the varying personalities and opinions involved in these projects. How do students prepare for a career in the game industry? How can instructors help them prepare?

Developing creativity and discipline skillsets is certainly a big part of the preparation process. But an even bigger part is acclimating students to the realization that the vast majority of their work in the game industry will involve interacting with other developers. Working on students' soft skills is crucial to their preparation for this career. Instructors can require students to workshop their assignments, review one another's work, and provide feedback. It's a good idea to incorporate at least one group project into each course.

Students need collaborative experiences, both to hone their soft skills and to have examples to talk about when interviewers ask what group projects they've worked on, how those went, what problems they encountered, and how they dealt with those problems. Those sorts of questions are frequently asked during game industry interviews; I've asked them of people as the interviewer and have answered them as an interviewee.

Individual projects can show a student's creativity and work ethic, but they don't tell employers anything about that person's ability to collaborate with others, a critical skill for success in the game industry. Putting students on teams simulates the real-world work environment. I've placed students on teams ranging from 3 to 25, with a wide range of results. But bigger isn't necessarily better. The best game I've seen from a student team came from one with only 8 students on it (kudos to the *Arpeggio* team!). These group projects are the sorts of experiences game industry interviewers want to hear about.

Look to build team projects into game design classes as much as possible. Such experiences are more valuable than grades in determining someone's aptitude for the kinds of creativity and interactions the game industry wants to see.

CHAPTER 8

Game Genres and Their Players

GENRE EXPECTATIONS

Every game falls into at least one genre. Some crossover games fall into two or more. The game *10,000,000* combines elements of endless runners, match-3, and role-playing games (RPGs). *Epistory* combines aspects of action–adventure games, RPGs, and typing tutors. Even games that deliver completely new types of gameplay belong to a genre, one that they have forged themselves.

It's vital for game developers, especially narrative designers, to know what genre(s) their game fits into. Is it a first-person shooter (FPS), adventure game, platformer, or some innovative combination of multiple genres? The answer dictates the path the game's development should take.

Likewise, it's important for game design students to think about the genre(s) into which their games fit, what that genre's players expect of those sorts of games, and where their games will meet or exceed those expectations (or turn the expectations on their heads).

Every established genre has certain standards of gameplay, control schemes, story, user interface, tropes, and so on. The developers crafting a game within a genre need to be very aware of those standards. Taking a genre in a new direction while retaining connections to genre standards can revitalize a genre that was getting stale, for both players and developers. Every game should look to add something new to its genre, even if it's just a small twist on an existing game mechanic.

Think of mobile games. Match-3 games like the massively successful *Candy Crush* and its many clones showcase simple gameplay that engages players for a while. But there's only so much of that gameplay most players can take before it grows old. A game like *10,000,000* takes the match-3 gameplay and uses it as the base, then mixes in elements of a dungeon-crawling RPG and an endless runner. Other mobile games start with match-3 and add strategy game mechanics, a social/Massively Multiplayer Online (MMO) framework, or other ideas borrowed from successful competitors. Layering new gameplay elements onto simple mechanics keeps players engaged much longer than repeating what's already familiar. Big-budget console games have more moving pieces, but they layer in ideas from other genres as well: How many action games now feature RPG elements like an inventory and skill trees?

Below you'll find a list of some major game genres, the game mechanics that are core to each, and what players seem to want from that type of game. Many of these categories overlap, so lots of games would fall into more than one genre.

If you're an instructor, you can approach this as a classroom activity: Have students name genres and the core gameplay of each, then write them on a whiteboard. You'll easily fill up a wall before students run out of ideas. Note that opinions about which core mechanics are most crucial to the player experience in a certain genre will often vary from person to person; my lists below are based on my interests and experiences playing these games, and they might vary greatly from the list anyone else would come up with. Treat my lists as examples.

RPGs (The *Elder Scrolls* series, *The Witcher 3: Wild Hunt*, *Fallout: New Vegas*):

- Core mechanics—story, combat, exploration, character development.
- Players want an intensely social, collaborative experience, either with real people (in tabletop RPGs) or realistic-seeming non-player characters (digital RPGs), in a deep game world with a rich story.

Platformers (*Super Mario Odyssey, Rayman Legends*):

- Core mechanics—movement around the level, puzzles, and physical challenges.
- Players want a fast-moving, fun experience that provides constant challenge and reward.

Strategy Games (*Age of Empires, Starcraft*):

- Core mechanics—building, resource-gathering, tech trees, variety of units, combat.

- Players want a wide range of strategies to use in different situations, as well as a feeling of mastering the tactics available to each side.

Racing Games:

- There are two distinct types of racing games—arcade and simulation.
  - Simulation (*Gran Turismo, Forza*):
    - Core mechanics—vehicle building and upgrading, realistic tracks, and car parameters.
    - Players want to feel like they're really driving race cars that they may never see in real life. They want an experience as close to the real thing as possible.
  - Arcade (*Mario Kart, Cruisin' USA*):
    - Core mechanics—fast, fun, wahoo action, lots of interaction among players.
    - Players want a fun, social experience with lots of opportunities to interact with their friends while playing.

MOBAs (Multiplayer Online Battle Arenas; *League of Legends, DOTA 2*):

- Core mechanics – hero abilities, map layout, lane tactics, and team composition.

- Players want fast-paced combat, strong team interactions, a wide variety of heroes to choose from, and fluid gameplay.

MMOs (Massively Multiplayer Online RPGs; *World of Warcraft, Final Fantasy XIV, EVE Online*):

- Core mechanics—social interactions (guilds, raids, etc.), crafting, combat, level grinding, exploration, role-playing.

- Note that MMOs require vast game worlds and engaging content to keep players online for a long time. Thus, these games use many layers of core mechanics that can hook many different types of players.

- Players want a more social experience (or else they'd play a single-player RPG rather than an MMO); they want challenging combat with diverse "builds" and ways to play, strong role-playing and character-building elements, rare items and lucky drops, cooperation or rivalry with other groups of players, and a giant world to explore.

Horror (*Silent Hill, Amnesia: The Dark Descent*):

- Core mechanics—combat and/or puzzles, frequent surprises, a mysterious story with twists and shocking moments.

- Players want to experience shock and dread, confront the unexpected, and uncover the secrets of a forbidding environment. These games are almost always solo experiences to enhance the fright factor.

Action/Adventure (*Uncharted, Tomb Raider, Batman: Arkham City*):

- Core mechanics—exploration, story, character interactions, combat, and/or puzzles and challenges.

- Players want an exciting, extensive world to explore, interesting characters to meet, engaging challenges, and an engrossing story.

Those are just a few examples of game genres, the core mechanics that define them, and what keeps players coming back for more. Your own list will vary. Note also that many games nowadays are hybrids, incorporating mechanics from two or more genres.

Here's the point: Your game's genre determines its core feature set. As you conceptualize your game, figure out where it fits into your own genre breakdown, and what groups of players it will appeal to. That should focus your planning and development efforts.

You should regularly review your design during development, as the process of implementation inevitably causes some drift away from the original intent. This can result in a loss of focus and weakening of the concept's core appeal. This is especially true on large teams, as the game design changes a little bit every day.

You'll need to recalibrate often to keep everyone headed in the same direction. It takes a conscious effort, exerted at multiple points during the game's development, to maintain focus. But it pays off: Great games are the ones that stick to their core elements and polish them until they shine.

Working on this process in game design and narrative design classes is crucial. These classes should instill the habits needed for a successful career in the game industry. One of those habits is constant analysis of your design plans (and those of the team). Practice introspection as you go through the revision cycle: create, show, get feedback, revise, and repeat. That's the loop that effective developers follow.

CHAPTER 9

The Game Development Process

How do teams, players, and game genres come together in the process of creating a game? Let's take a look at digital development then move on to analog game development in Chapter 10.

DIGITAL GAME DEVELOPMENT—PRE-PRODUCTION

We've discussed the fact that all games begin with an idea and that ideas can come from anywhere. Get out of your comfort zone: Find inspiration elsewhere and bring it into the gaming realm!

But when you're on a development team, the starting point for the game might not be your ideas, or even the ideas of others on the team. The company you work for may have the rights to develop a game based on a book, movie, or TV series, and they task your team with developing a game based on that intellectual property (IP). When I was at Volition, the company was then owned by THQ, which had the rights to develop a game based on the *Punisher* comic books. We came up with a game concept that used that IP, presented our ideas to company management, and developed the *Punisher* video game from that start. Other times, a company will solicit game concepts from employees, gathering ideas and sifting through them to find one or more that seem promising. That process resulted in the first *Saints Row* game for Volition, the start of a long-running and very successful franchise.

But when you're a lone developer (or a student in a game design class), it's up to you to come up with the initial concept for your game. Once you have that idea, think about the elements that will help turn it into a game design. It is very helpful to use a concept document template (see Appendix C) at this point to formalize your ideas and explain them to others. This step shows you've thought about how to develop your idea and how saleable it is. A well-written concept doc is a great portfolio piece to showcase your creativity to potential employers.

Once you've written up a concept doc, get feedback on your ideas. In my game design and narrative design classes, students write up one-page concepts and present them to others in small workshop groups. Everyone reads and reacts to the concepts of others. Students use what they read in others' concepts to refine their own work; borrowing ideas from others is a time-honored tradition in the game industry. (*Mortal Kombat* wouldn't exist without *Street Fighter*, and *Candy Crush* wouldn't exist without *Bejeweled*.) If you're working on a game on your own, you need to find friends, family, or other gamers who'll read your concept and give you feedback on it.

At every step of the game-development process, employ the revision cycle to refine your work. The sooner you get feedback that helps you find flaws in your game design, the faster and easier it is for you to fix them and move on.

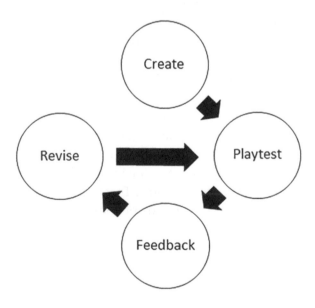

After creating and refining your concept document, the next stage is to expand it into a Game Design Document (GDD) that will take your game concepts to the next level (see Appendix C). This template's instructions lead you through the process of planning out your game's design. If you look over the template, you'll see sections in which to develop your game's story, setting (game world), gameplay, art style, and initial thoughts on your game's aural environment (sound and music).

A GDD of 20–40 pages is generally a sufficient jumping-off point for a game development team. More than that is usually wasted effort. Overly long GDDs will confuse or bore the same team members who should be the game's most passionate advocates. Remember: You're barely off the starting line. There's months or years of development to come, countless decisions to be made (including ones that haven't even occurred to you at this point), and many, many changes that the game's design must go through before you cross the finish line.

Keep your GDD (or the wiki that develops from it) as streamlined as you can while still conveying the info the team needs to start developing the game. In the late 1800s, the Prussian general Helmuth von Moltke said, "No plan survives contact with the enemy." Remember that quote. The GDD is your battle plan and the "enemy" is implementation. Once you start creating your game in a game engine, your plans are going to change. Some of your favorite ideas will prove too hard to implement. Or you'll start to implement something and a better method will occur to someone on the team. Or the entire focus of the game will change.

In short, the game you ship may be very different from the one in your GDD. Recognize the GDD for what it is—your game's starting point—and don't spend too much time over-developing it. Get into the implementation phase and see where your creativity takes you.

The designer who writes up the GDD is never an expert in all aspects of game development. The narrative designer, for example, is the team's story expert. The lead game designer is the team's gameplay expert. The art lead is the visual expert on the team. And so on. On a team with different people fulfilling all these functions, filling out the GDD is a group effort. Meetings and brainstorming sessions hash out the rough outlines of the GDD's content. The narrative designer (or another team member) writes this up into a first pass at the game's GDD. Cycles of comments from all parties involved, revisions, and further meetings expand the GDD.

Once the GDD reaches a stage that feels like a solid foundation for the game's development, various team leads turn their sections into discipline-specific documents. The art lead takes the Art and Aesthetics section and develops that into an art style guide. The lead game designer takes the Gameplay section and turns that into a much more detailed document that describes the game systems and mechanics in great detail. The lead programmer develops a technical design document that lays out how the game's mechanics will be coded, along with file-naming formats, game engine specifics, and anything else the team's coders will need to create the technical foundation upon which the game will be built. The lead sound designer may take the Sound and Music section and go into much greater detail on these elements in a document for members of the audio team.

Many of these discipline-specific documents, along with the current version of the GDD, are put onto the pages of an internal wiki available to all team members. Often one person from each discipline team is tasked with maintaining and updating that team's section of the wiki as everyone shifts from pre-production to implementation.

MARKETING/AUDIENCE INFO

Every concept doc and GDD should contain at least a line or two about the game's intended audience. That determines almost everything about the game's content. If you are working on an AAA game, the publisher will have a marketing department that determines how to reach the target audience. But if you're an individual developer or you work for a small game company that publishes its own games, you need to think about how to reach your audience. You also need to do a competitive analysis, taking time to consider who else is in the game space you're aiming at, what games you'll be competing with, and so on. These developers should add a detailed Marketing Analysis section to their GDDs.

As an instructor or student in game design and narrative design classes, it is a good idea to create at least one GDD with a marketing section, to show that you're considering the competitive marketplace your game might enter. This is also a section in which you can discuss the ways your game will differ from ones that are already published in that genre. My concept doc templates include a small section for students to mention their game's USPs (Unique Selling Points). That's where they highlight the ways in which their game will expand its intended genre, presenting players with experiences they haven't seen yet.

DIGITAL GAME DEVELOPMENT—IMPLEMENTATION

When pre-production comes to a close, it's time to really get to work. The whole pre-production process is maybe 5% of all the effort that goes into making a digital game (or an analog game, for that matter). Usually the pre-pro period of initial planning for the game is done by a small team, sometimes just a few senior developers. These senior folks often become the leads of their disciplines once pre-production ends and production begins. That's the point when most of the rest of the team arrives, switching over from the previous game they were working on.

Before pre-pro is done, the leads also need to create pipelines for the work to be done by the developers within their discipline. This includes interdependencies between different departments: tasks that need to be handed off between different teams to be completed. Producers, the overseers of the game's production schedule, help organize this.

For example, the character design pipeline begins with a game designer writing a brief description of a monster or non-player character (NPC) the game needs. A concept artist takes that description and draws a sketch of the character. Then a character modeler (artist) creates a sprite (for a 2D game) or model (for a 3D game) from that sketch. It then goes to a rigger to place bones within the model, then to an animator to add movement to the figure. Usually, a sound designer is involved as well, to add sound effects to the character's movement (such as footsteps, the rustle of cloth, and creaking of leather and armor). And at every stage of this character's development, appropriate leads review its progress and either make suggestions for revision or OK it to proceed to the next stage.

Production pipelines are often represented visually by a Gantt chart (or some other means). These charts graphically represent the timeline of work needed to accomplish every task required to complete the game. Since all but the simplest games consist of thousands of individual tasks, worked on by dozens and sometimes hundreds of developers, Gantt charts can get very complex indeed. It's one of the jobs of producers to create these charts with the help of discipline leads, who better understand how long each step in a development process should take. Then the game's producers need to keep track of progress of each task during development, spot any problems as early as possible, and work with leads and developers to work out solutions.

ID	Task Name	Predecessors	Duration	Jul 23, '06							Jul 30, '06							Aug 6, '06							Aug 13, '06						
				S	M	T	W	T	F	S	S	M	T	W	T	F	S	S	M	T	W	T	F	S	S	M	T	W	T	F	S
1	Start		0 days																												
2	a	1	4 days																												
3	b	1	5.33 days																												
4	c	2	5.17 days																												
5	d	2	6.33 days																												
6	e	3,4	5.17 days																												
7	f	5	4.5 days																												
8	g	6	5.17 days																												
9	Finish	7,8	0 days																												

Courtesy of Dbshear on Wikipedia. https://en.wikipedia.org/wiki/Gantt_chart

Once the pre-production stage of a game's development is over, the team starts growing. The senior developers now transition from their pre-pro roles into their team lead roles. As developers are added to the discipline teams within the project, the leads take on more management tasks, doling out work to those in their groups, coordinating with producers on workflow and pipelines, and getting the new members of their teams up to speed on the project's needs and tools.

Even after implementation begins, pre-production tasks may still be underway. There are almost always changes to the game's story (sometimes daily) as designers implement the game's design. Cinematic scripts that were written during pre-pro are often changed as the game evolves. Design plans are revised and characters re-envisioned. Ideally, these changes are noted in the game's GDD or internal wiki pages, but often they are made rapidly, by many people, and the former documents quickly become dated.

Most of the effort at this stage is in implementing the game's design with the engine and editor chosen for development. Level designers build the terrain and environments; artists create characters, buildings, vehicles, and props; game designers put characters and events into the game and add scripting to bring the world to life; sound designers create sound effects and ambient sounds; composers make music that adds emotion and atmosphere to the game; coders write tools and engine add-ons to enhance the team's workflow.

All of this work involves negotiating thousands of interdependencies among tasks and disciplines. Game designers can't get gameplay in until level designers have created (or at least roughly whiteboxed) the game's environments. Level designers need buildings and terrain pieces (trees, bushes, boulders, etc.) from artists to create those environments. Sound designers need characters, events, and environments in place before they can evaluate sound effects and music. Digital game development involves thousands of parts moving simultaneously. It's like trying to assemble a puzzle on a moving train as the pieces bounce around on the table.

As the developers build content, there's also usually an internal Quality Assurance (QA) group playtesting the game and giving feedback and suggestions. Many companies have their own QA departments working alongside their development teams. This adds to development costs but greatly improves the game's quality, as it creates a rapid, continual revision cycle that markedly improves the player experience. When I worked at Volition, QA was a separate department; when I was at Zenimax Online, working on the *Elder Scrolls Online*, QA was integrated with the development team, with several QAers working alongside designers, artists, and the rest of the developers.

A digital game will pass through the following stages during production:

- **First Playable/Prototype:** At this point, the game is still incomplete, but it's playable enough to get a firm idea of the player experience. Only some of the game mechanics are working, and only certain sections of the game world have been roughed in. In these areas, generic blocks take the place of buildings and other features, dropped in just for quick testing of gameplay.

- **Alpha:** This is the first "complete" version of the game. All game mechanics are at least roughed in (some with temporary workarounds while final code or assets are still in progress), and the entire game world is traversable. There's still a lot of content yet to be added, but a true sense of the gameplay and player experience can now be had.

  The Alpha stage is also when companies often decide to open up playtesting to people outside the company. This could be a series of small focus groups of five to ten people who are invited to the company's offices to playtest the game while team members silently observe. Or it could be an Alpha test open to hundreds of players, all of whom playtest from home while the team watches gameplay and responds to feedback.

  This is how you collect vital feedback. As we discussed earlier, really listening and responding to these suggestions is critical. Ignoring playtester feedback usually only makes a game worse. I saw it happen firsthand when I was part of a large Massively Multiplayer Online (MMO) development team. Internal feedback, QA feedback, and playtester feedback were often ignored during development, much to the game's detriment. We repeatedly commented that dialogue was too long, scripted sequences were boring lore dumps, and that staples of the MMO genre that were functioning in the game (such as a minimap and scrolling combat text) were being removed at the whim of the creative director. These were all bad calls and the game paid the price. Fans and reviewers criticized the game for these and many other problems upon release. Judgment of the final product was harsh. Our score on Metacritic—an online review aggregator—was in the low 70s, which is considered poor for a big-budget, AAA release. After numerous patches and revisions, the game now reviews decently (in the low 80s), but the poor reception and sales at launch could have been avoided if team management listened to the feedback it got prior to release.

- **Beta:** When a game's mechanics are all in and functioning mostly as intended, the game has reached Beta stage. Though much polishing and tweaking remains to be done, all content has been added to the game. Many companies hold off on focus testing and open testing until the Beta stage out of worry that an alpha would make a poor first impression on the public and press.

  Beta is also the point at which "feature freeze" should occur, enforced by the game's producer. Once the freeze is announced, no one can add to features or mechanics to the game. The most critical factor in a game's quality isn't how many mechanics it has, but how well its existing mechanics work. The freeze helps you polish what you've got without the risk of a last-minute addition upsetting the apple cart.

  MMO games work differently. They take a very long time to create—five or six years of work by a team of hundreds—because they need many different mechanics to appeal to a wide variety of players. The mechanics also need to be involved enough to hook players long-term. That's the only way for the publisher to recoup their development investment.

  The Beta marks when a game should really come together, when its scope is complete and gameplay is finalized. There's still a lot of bug-fixing and polishing to go, but the end is in sight. At this stage, the QA team shifts into top gear, hunting down as many bugs as possible while also pointing out any aspect of the game that feels unpolished.

- **Release Candidate:** This stage is critical for video games that need to be submitted to the first-party company—the company that makes the hardware on which the game will be published (e.g., Nintendo, Sony, Microsoft). These games need to be submitted to the appropriate platform makers for approval to be published.

  For games that will be published on Steam (or another service) or self-published, this stage represents the team's proposed candidate for publication, submitted to company management for review and approval. If it passes muster, the game gets published or goes through a review process if being released on a third-party service.

  For console and multiplatform games, this review is a major hurdle to clear. The proposed candidate is submitted to the publisher's compliance testing department, where it's checked against literally thousands of criteria. These are spelled out in submission documentation from the publisher, with lists of bugs organized into groups by severity. Even a single major bug (A-level) can get a game immediately kicked out of compliance testing and sent back to the developer for fixing. An example of an A-level bug is what's called a soft-crash—the player character is alive but unable to advance past a certain point in the game. Anyplace where the game's framerate drops below the acceptable minimum can be considered a B-level bug. A few B-level bugs end testing and require a game to be fixed and then resubmitted.

  Once the bugs are deemed fixed by the developer, the game is resubmitted and testing begins again. If severe bugs are found again, the testers kick the game back to the developer for further fixes, and the cycle continues. Game developers often have stories of nightmare submission processes that took months before the game was finally approved (or the game developer gave up on it).

- **Master/Gold:** This is essentially the final, approved release candidate. When company management and third-party platform owners (in the case of console games or games released on Steam and other services) are satisfied with the most recent version of the game, that becomes the Master (or Gold) version and the game is set to be published. Time to celebrate!

For non-console games, there's usually still bug-fixing, patching, and updating to come, but most of the team moves on. They might transfer over to a sequel to the just-released game (said sequel should have been undergoing pre-production with a small team while the previous game was still three to four months from release; see the pre-production stage above) or they might be moving on to a completely different game. For most games, a few members in each discipline may stay on the project for updates and maintenance, but it's a wrap for the rest of the team. For a blockbuster game that the company wants to keep customers playing, a larger team would stay on to frequently release new content and bug fixes.

FOR STUDENTS AND INSTRUCTORS IN CLASSROOMS

Given the complex, iterative, and interactive nature of the game development process, it's crucial for courses in game design to simulate this environment as closely and as often as possible. I recommend having at least one project in which students work collaboratively in groups of three to four.

It's also vital for game design programs to include a class in which students work on large teams, spending a semester or two creating a game. This is a great simulation of a game development environment that forces students to face the issues inherent in collaborating with a large group of co-workers. On these projects, one or a few students should assume positions of responsibility within the team (creative director, producer, discipline leads, etc.). This further helps students acclimate to the structure of a game development team.

In my experience mentoring large student teams, any group larger than 15 or so becomes unwieldy. The creative director and producer roles are positions of authority that can be hard for students to pull off on a team of their peers. Student producers and creative directors have trouble keeping teams greater than 15 or so on track, holding everyone accountable for the progress of the project. In larger teams, slackers begin to slip through the cracks, letting more dedicated students take on heavier workloads while they coast along. The larger the team, the greater the risk of imbalances like these, and the harder it is for instructors to catch them.

This is exacerbated by the need for these student teams to do work outside of the classroom on their projects. No project will make decent headway with students spending only three or so hours a week on it, so team members need to get together outside of class to work.

Game development teams are complex, multi-headed beasts. The sooner students learn their role in such a team—by collaborating effectively and communicating with those in other disciplines—the better they'll adapt to life in the industry. Team projects are therefore essential learning tools. Just be careful how you organize them.

CHAPTER 10

Writing and Design for Analog Games

H OW DOES THE PROCESS of writing and design for analog games differ from that for digital games? First, a bit of background.

The first five years of my career in the game industry were devoted almost exclusively to analog games. I worked on *Dungeons & Dragons*® and *Advanced Dungeons & Dragons*® products—adventure modules, hardback books, monster compendia, etc.—as well as products in other role-playing lines and board games. I contributed to over 90 games in all, for TSR and Milton Bradley. Even though most of my career has been devoted to digital games, analog games still hold a fond place in my heart.

Courtesy of Wikimedia.org.

Many famous video game developers got their start in analog games, and analog game conventions have clearly been transported into the digital realm. If you look at a photo of miniatures arranged on a tabletop during a fantasy role-playing game (RPG) battle and then at a photo of the action in a digital game like *Diablo*, the similarities are striking. The combat systems used in video games came directly from those mechanics in tabletop games. Modern game mechanics, dungeon design, and character progression all derive from ideas in tabletop games. Digital games owe a huge debt to their analog predecessors, and it's worth studying the latter as you design the former.

SIMILARITIES AND DIFFERENCES

Consider the process of pre-production. Many tasks in this stage barely differ in analog and digital projects. Each should start with a brief concept document that lays out just the essence of the game's story, how it works, where it's set, and so on. The concept doc for an analog game bears a very strong resemblance to that of an equivalent digital game (see Appendix C for templates to create concept documents for digital and analog games).

When you take the game design to the next stage, whether it's a Game Design Document (GDD) or some other means of formalizing your plans, the paths begin to diverge. The Story section and the Game World section of each GDD would be the same; the Game World section would as well. But the Gameplay sections, while featuring similar systems (the "what" of the game—what the player can do in the game), would introduce very different mechanics (the "how" of the game systems—how they actually work in the game). An RPG might have a character creation screen with many under-the-hood calculations, but the analog game's character creation mechanics could involve players rolling dice to determine stats.

Likewise, the descriptions of the game world would be very similar in the documentation for an analog game and its digital equivalent, but the implementation of that world would differ greatly. An analog game would have a board or other playing surface with physical maps and layouts of the terrain as players explored. These would be fully described in the GDD. The digital version would list assets needed to create the game world, means to prevent players from moving too quickly across the world (speeding past carefully crafted content), and so on.

But the processes in creating digital and analog games also differ in many ways. Even during the pre-production process, digital games have a tech lead who works to create a Technical Design Document from the starting point given by the GDD (or equivalent wiki). There's also an art lead who works on an Art Style Guide for the project, and so on.

Along with regular art staff, analog games also often have graphic artists who work on maps, formatting rulebooks, and creating other components of the game. These physical components of analog games are equivalent to the user interface (UI) of digital games—the health bars, minimap, radar, skill buttons, etc. that remain onscreen during gameplay.

The UI in a computer or console game tells players what they need to know in any situation. The UI presented to players during combat may differ from what they see during conversations with NPCs or while perusing their inventory. To keep the UI simple, it communicates only what players need to know in their current circumstances.

The physical components of an analog game serve the same purpose. The game board, cards, pieces, and other components are carefully designed to fit the game's subject and tone while conveying specific information to the player. The game designer works with the artist and the graphic designer to plan every component and assess how each fits with all the other pieces of the game. Developers must practice intentional design to ensure that every part of an analog game helps create an engaging experience.

SPECIAL DESIGN CONSIDERATIONS FOR ANALOG GAMES

While digital games include sounds, music, and visuals that analog games don't have to deal with, analog games have unique considerations of their own. Analog games are designed to bring friends together around a table. Encouraging interaction among players is critical to their design and should be the foremost concern in the minds of those who create board games, card games, and tabletop RPGs.

Think about the thousands of years that people have been creating and playing games. Before digital games captured the popular imagination, almost no games were designed to be played solo. There was Solitaire, and there were a few variants of little boards with a bunch of pegs and an open hole. That's about it. Analog games were not made for solo players.

Compare that to digital games. The vast majority are designed for individuals playing in front of a computer or TV screen by themselves. Sure, some digital party games and fighting games work best with two or more people around, but most video games are solo affairs. Digital RPGs and

Massively Multiplayer Online (MMO) games simulate social interactions by adding non-player characters (NPCs) to game worlds or allowing hordes of anonymous players into a game, but interactions are limited compared to the experience of playing analog games with friends.

Courtesy of Wikimedia Commons. https://commons. wikimedia.org/wiki/File:Family_playing_a_board_game_(2).jpg

That social element is the greatest strength of analog games; it should be played up for all it's worth. Build as much player interaction into your game as you can. It increases player enjoyment, builds camaraderie, and keeps players coming back for more. Every game mechanic should be crafted with the goal of increasing player interactions. This also encourages emergent gameplay, with players adding content, creating house rules, and finding ways to play your game that you never expected.

For a game designer, players' ability to create surprising gameplay and to find rule holes you never knew existed can be exasperating, amusing, and illuminating all at once. It's embarrassing to see reviewers and players posting about bugs and holes that they've found. It's a grin-and-bear-it situation, as all you can do is resolve not to make those mistakes again. Treat it as a learning experience and move on. (Though the learning to be had here is generally summed up as "do more playtesting!")

A critical design consideration in analog games is determining the balance between random chance and player skill. You need both in your game design, but striking the correct balance is crucial.

Randomness adds tension to gameplay, making sure that players are never certain how an action or battle will turn out. Rolling dice or using other means of generating random numbers is a staple in analog games because it's such an easy means of varying the outcome of player actions. There's also a tactile thrill in handling and rolling dice. Rolling dice around in your hands and casting them onto the table (or shuffling and dealing out cards) forges a physical connection that engages players with your game. Don't underestimate that connection.

Courtesy of Wikipedia. https://en.wikipedia.org/wiki/Dice

Different dice serve different purposes in game design. When you want a number of outcomes to have an equal chance of occurring, have the player roll a single die. A six-sided die (d6) would give six outcomes an equal chance (16.67% apiece) to occur. If there are lots of potential outcomes with equal chances of occurring, use a bigger die (a d20, for example). If you want a distribution of chances for various events, use multiple dice. When you roll two six-sided dice (2d6s), instead of six outcomes each with an equal chance of occurring, you get 11 outcomes (rolling 2d6s gives you a result from 2 to 12) with some much more likely to happen than others. A result of 2 or 12 happens only 1 in 36 (2.8%) times you roll 2d6s, but a result of 7 occurs 1 time in every 6 rolls (16.67%). Using multiple dice in your game gives you a random element, but also helps you make some results more likely than others, often an important consideration in game design.

The other side of the coin is the effect of player skill. As randomness serves to increase uncertainty in gameplay, player skill decreases it. As a player's mastery of your gameplay increases, they become better able to shift gameplay outcomes in their favor. Allowing player skill (and player character ability increases) to modify die rolls in their favor boosts their confidence and enhances their enjoyment of your game. As a designer, you want players to feel a sense of mastery over simpler game mechanics while maintaining uncertainty with more complex mechanics and random factors that player skill can ameliorate but never eliminate.

The games of chess and *Candyland* differ in many respects. The most fundamental difference in gameplay is that the result of a chess game is determined entirely by player skill, while that of *Candyland* is entirely based on chance. The four-year-olds who love *Candyland* have no clue that their frequent wins have nothing to do with any degree of skill at the game. Eventually children move on to more sophisticated games that require more reasoning and skill. As you look to appeal to more mature audiences, randomness gives way to a higher skill ceiling, but in most games never disappears entirely.

CHAPTER 11

Writing Advice

I'D LIKE TO PASS along some lessons I've learned in my years as a narrative designer. Some of this advice is specific to games and some is for writing in general. These are all strategies that have worked for me. I hope some of them strike a chord with you.

Writing is an act of communication between the writer and reader. Writers who don't keep the reader in mind (just as with game designers who don't keep the player in mind) are missing much of the intent behind the act of writing.

Samuel Johnson (1709–1784), the creator of the first successful English dictionary, once said, "A writer only begins a book. A reader finishes it" That quote concisely sums up the relationship between the writer and reader—a writer's work isn't done until someone has read it. Keeping that in mind helps the writer create for the reader's enjoyment and edification. Who is this game being created for, and what do they want from that experience? Keep those questions foremost in your mind as you undertake writing and design tasks. The answers to those questions should guide the writer in all aspects of story creation, character development, and plot points throughout the game's development.

Courtesy of Wikipedia.
https://en.wikipedia.org/
wiki/Samuel_Johnson

STORY AND GAMEPLAY

Always remember the functions a story should fulfill in a game, especially a digital game. The story needs to provide context for players, telling them why they matter in the game and why their actions matter. The story should motivate players to continue through the game, intriguing them so they always want to find out what might be around the next corner.

As mentioned earlier, story can also keep players going even when gameplay gets stale. Adding new characters, events, and game mechanics can be very expensive in terms of developer time and asset creation. With an engaging story, however, players will continue playing just to see where the story takes them next.

That being said, in almost all games the function of story is to support the intended gameplay. Players play games to actively participate in the action, not to read or be talked at endlessly. Story should supplement gameplay, not overwhelm it. The two should dovetail nicely together, with gameplay leading the way and story as a loyal supporter.

One genre of games where these roles are usually reversed is role-playing games (RPGs). In these games, story takes top billing. Players are there to see how the story develops around them, to take their character from humble beginnings to great glory, to achieve some ultimate goal. In RPGs, gameplay serves as the vehicle that conveys the player character (and player) from plot point to plot point in an engaging story. The gameplay still needs to satisfy the player's need for action and excitement, but the allure of an RPG is more the story than the gameplay.

HOW WRITING STORIES FOR GAMES DIFFERS

One high hurdle for writers coming to games from other media is that the story is no longer theirs. When an author writes a novel, they own that story. Others can give feedback or request changes, but the story comes from the writer and it belongs very much to them. It feels like it's theirs, with others contributing to it.

It's different for games. Here the story belongs to the game and the team and depends on the intended gameplay. Some writers from other media find it difficult to deal with this loss of control over the story. I've seen writers from other industries fail to make the transition to games for this reason. Clashes with game designers, sound designers, artists, programmers, and others with a stake in the direction of the story are common when a writer doesn't accept the reality of writing for games.

Another complication arises from the story's dependence on gameplay. During development, a game's design changes every day, for many different reasons. Sometimes the changes are small; sometimes they are major upheavals. But the story and characters need to adapt to each one. So part of the narrative designer's job is to keep track of changes that come from dozens or sometimes hundreds of developers.

The story isn't yours, and game elements outside the purview of the story often require it to change daily; these are the aspects of narrative design that drive writers from other industries up the wall. Make sure that you're willing to work under those conditions before diving into a career as a narrative designer.

Another issue that writers in the game industry contend with is the high cost of dialogue. When you're writing a novel, an additional word is just another word, a bit of additional space in the book. But when you write for games, every word of spoken dialogue costs money, and any line that doesn't advance the story or gameplay must be ruthlessly culled.

In games, dialogue is either text on the screen or it's voiced by voice actors. In either case, it's critical for the game's narrative designer to bevigilant in keeping dialogue crisp and concise.

Don't test the patience of your player/reader, even when the words onscreen aren't voiced. To speak with a non-player character (NPC), they need to move their player character (PC) up to the character, interact with them, read the dialogue box that pops up, and finally digest that information. It had better be worth the effort! If you waste too much of the player's time with NPCs who have nothing of consequence to say, soon they'll start skipping in-game conversations, and miss out on the ones that are critical to gameplay or story.

One example of this happened early in my tenure at Volition (makers of the *Red Faction* series, the *Saints Row* series, and many other games). I was working as the narrative designer for the first *Red Faction* game, while another team was working on a fantasy RPG. This was slated to be a PS2-release day game, coming out when the PS2 appeared in stores, whereas *Red Faction* wasn't due to be released for months afterward. So there was a lot of pressure to get that RPG done on time.

I was called in to help out with the narrative design a couple of times as the deadline neared. When I looked at the writing, I noticed that many of the NPC dialogues ran over the first text box, requiring the player to press a button again to see the remaining text in a second box (the game's dialogue wasn't voiced, just text on the screen). Often, the excess text was just a word or two. I pointed this out to the game's writer, mentioning how irritating it would be for players to continually press an extra button just to get another word of dialogue. This was brushed off with a shrug. I later mentioned that I was being careful to keep all my dialogue extra short to avoid running over into a second box. Again there was a shrug.

When PS2 launch day arrived and the game came out, reviewers and the public noticed. One critic used the phrase "stupefyingly overwritten." The game itself was a critical and financial failure. You can't pin it all on the story, but I think at least part of the negative reaction came from the game's lack of consideration for the time and patience of players.

Games in which the dialogue isn't voiced need to be careful about excess verbiage. But in games with voice acting, the problem is much worse. Consider all the steps involved in getting voiced dialogue into a game. The narrative designer writes it. It's added the game so playtesters can react to it. Sometimes this involves a sound designer running the lines through a text-to-speech process to convert the written words into robo-speech (like your GPS's speech, only worse). Then the writer has to seek out fellow developers and Quality Assurance (QA) for feedback on the lines. The writer plays through the game themselves, listening to lines and re-writing ones that don't ring true. At some companies I've worked for, I would prowl around the studio, grabbing random developers (artists, programmers) and dragging them into a small recording studio we'd set up. They'd voice the lines to the best of their ability, and those voice files would be sent over to sound designers and imported into the game. Those were just temporary recordings to get lines listened to more closely during testing (and to short-circuit complaints about awful robo-voices). At Raven Software, we went a step further and paid theatre professors and grad students at the nearby University of Wisconsin to come in and voice lines.

And all of that time spent is just the tip of the iceberg. There are rounds of feedback and revision of the voiced lines during development. Focus groups play the game and their feedback affects the game's dialogue. Gameplay changes necessitate re-writing and re-recording. Then, as the game nears its release deadline, professional voice actors are auditioned, their recordings are reviewed by the narrative designer and other developers, and actors are picked for all the voice roles within the game. That's when things start to get really expensive.

Once the real voice actors are chosen and recording sessions are set up, it's off to LA (usually) for the narrative designer. There they join up with a voice director and one or more studio technicians to guide the voice actors through the recording sessions. Those sessions run eight hours a day for one or more weeks (the recording sessions for *Red Faction Guerrilla*, the third game in the *Red Faction* series, went for over five weeks). Professional voice actors cost more than $400 per hour. Then there's the cost of renting the recording studio and paying the technician and voice director. The game development company also pays for the narrative designer's time, hotel room, food, car rental, and other expenses.

Once the lines are recorded, someone has to sort through the takes of each line, choosing the best one and marking it for the sound designer back at home. They also turn the best take of each line into a separate audio file, name it according to an agreed-upon convention, and add the file into the correct directory in the game's file structure.

The testing and revision process isn't over. Lines are found that, despite the best efforts of everyone involved, were poorly recorded, badly voiced, or missed the needed emotional context. There are also lines that need to be re-recorded due to changes to the game's design during the recording sessions. Pickup voice recording sessions are generally scheduled for a month or more after the major sessions, just for the purpose of recording lines that were missed, changed, or need to be re-done for some other reason. And that session entails many of the same costs as the original voice sessions.

To give you an idea of the scale of efforts involved here, for the first *Red Faction* game, I wrote roughly 2,500 voiced dialogue lines. We drove up to a recording studio two hours away in Chicago and spent a few days recording those lines with dozens of voice actors. (One of the voice actors who had a minor part in the first *Red Faction* was Nolan North, who went on to play Nathan Drake in *Uncharted*.) A sound designer spent a few days at Volition cutting the lines and getting them into the game.

The third game in the *Red Faction* series—*Red Faction Guerrilla*—was a much costlier affair. It had over 32,000 voiced dialogue lines, written by me with the help of three interns. The voice recording sessions were done in LA, a massively more expensive location. We spent five weeks on the initial voice recording sessions and more than a week on the pickup sessions. I had several 100+ hour weeks preparing for those sessions in the month or so before leaving for LA. Given all the work done writing, re-writing, recording, testing, and re-recording during the development process, I believe their total cost was well over $1,000,000.

So, dialogue is expensive. It's imperative that narrative designers write as concisely as possible whether their game's dialogue is voiced or not. Ernest Hemingway's dialogue is a good model for game writers to emulate. In narrative design classes, I often contrast Hemingway's dialogue with student writing, and quite a contrast it is. Hemingway uses crisp dialogue lines and conversations that embody interactions between real-seeming people. Many students write conversations as a series of excruciatingly long dialogues; these are basically serial monologues in which characters take turns spewing long speeches at each other. That's neither good dialogue nor realistic conversation.

Here's a conversation from Hemingway's *The Sun Also Rises*:[1]

> Brett turned to Bill.
> "Have you been in this pestilential city long?"
> "Just got in today from Budapest."
> "How was Budapest?"
> "Wonderful. Budapest was wonderful."
> "Ask him about Vienna."
> "Vienna," said Bill, "is a strange city."
> "Very much like Paris," Brett smiled at him, wrinkling the corners of her eyes.
> "Exactly," Bill said. "Very much like Paris at this moment."
> "You *have* a good start."

That's the way conversations should flow, with characters actually listening to and responding to each other, moving at a brisk pace, and conveying intriguing content.

One of the reasons game writing gets a bad rap is the development process. Entire sections of games get removed, sometimes very late in development, due to a lack of resources. The corresponding story elements need to be shifted to other parts of the game, or removed and patched over. When characters are deleted from areas (or the entire game), a cascade of story changes often follows. Many times a game's story is essentially published in first-draft form: The narrative designer has been scrambling the whole time to patch the script together as design changes tear new holes in it.

Novels are written and re-written with the express intent of improving the story. But in games, changes to the script often stem from design considerations outside the realm of the story and can result in the story

---

[1] Hemingway, E. (1926; reprinted 1967). *The sun also rises*, Coles: London.

becoming less coherent with each change. The job of the narrative designer can feel like writing a story on the backs of puzzle pieces without seeing their fronts, then hoping the story makes sense when the pieces are all flipped over and the puzzle assembled.

HOW WRITING FOR GAMES IS THE SAME

Some elements of writing don't change. Revision is key to good writing of any type. As Hemingway reportedly said, "The first draft of anything is shit." This point holds for game writing as much as any other sort. Your first pass at dialogue and text for your game won't be great.

Game writers must learn to focus on the characters in their games' stories, rather than the events, because characters are what truly interest people. People care less about events than how characters react and change in response.

Game stories often get a bad rap because of the shallowness of players' ultimate goals. Tons of games present the player with "save the world" scenarios in which the PC is somehow the only person on Earth who can solve a certain problem. It's become a joke at this point. In the *Elder Scrolls Online* MMO, the game's central storyline involves the PC being told they are the only one who can save the continent of Tamriel from the demon prince Molag Bal. The game's core story drags players through quest after quest, leading up to the final confrontation in which they defeat Bal and banish him back to his home plane. They receive the title "Savior of Tamriel." They feel good about this for about 1.5 seconds until they get back to town and notice that everyone else in town has "Savior of Tamriel" hovering over their heads. So there's nothing special about them after all. They quietly remove that title from their character and continue playing.

Courtesy of SketchPort.org.

"Save the world" is a lazy goal for a game. Players can't rationally or emotionally relate to the experience of saving everything in the world. They just roll their eyes and play the game, hoping that at least the journey is fun because the end goal isn't interesting or realistic.

To avoid this problem, designers should make goals personal. You could save your hometown, rescue your best friend, or recover a puppy that the Big Bad has run away with. Come up with something meaningful to the PC, and it will become meaningful to players. Think about stories in acclaimed books, movies, or TV shows—apart from superhero movies, they're almost never about saving the world. Someone wants to stop the flow of drugs into their neighborhood, find out who killed their grandmother, or save the local elementary school from being shut down. Those are the sorts of goals players can relate to and get engaged in.

Another way that game stories are similar to those in other media is that storytelling techniques that have existed for thousands of years can be used to great effect in games. We can foreshadow upcoming events and places by letting the player hear hints or catch glimpses in the far distance. We can increase the difficulty of the tasks the player has to accomplish, putting ever more difficult tasks in from of them, to create rising action through the middle of the game. We add plot twists, sub-plots driven by NPCs, danger, and even character deaths to heighten the tension the player feels as they progress through the game.

Game stories not only pose unique challenges for narrative designers, but they also present opportunities to improve our craft and raise it to the level of the best writing in books, plays, movies, and other media.

CHAPTER 12

Teaching Narrative Design and Game Design

A S MUCH FUN AS it is to create games and write for them, I think I enjoy teaching game design and narrative design even more. I get to interact with engaged students, pass along the lessons I've learned from the game industry, and watch their creations come to life. I hope this book helps other instructors pick up lessons and tactics to use in their classrooms.

I try to convey the lessons I've learned in the game industry to my students. Thus, my class lessons and assignments reflect the actual work that game designers and narrative designers undertake on a daily basis. I believe that this is the most valuable content instructors can bring to students interested in these fields—information and skills that can help them get into the game industry and do well there. All the information contained in the following chapters comes from lessons used in my game design and narrative design classes. Also, see Appendices B and C for syllabi and assignment instructions and templates.

A carryover from my game industry experiences is to think of students as customers. My intention is to deliver as valuable a learning experience as I can. Just as a game player's experience is the primary consideration for all design and narrative elements, the student experience in a course should guide every aspect of that course.

All my classes involve collaborative activities among students. In the first class meeting, I tell students that my classes are PVE

(Player vs. Environment) settings, not PVP (Player vs. Player). Virtually all the students have played Massively Multiplayer Online role-playing games (MMO RPGs), and they instantly get the reference. Gaming terminology helps students understand the classroom as a collaborative environment, not a competitive one. Every student is expected to help everyone else in the class master the course material; the goal is to work together to achieve their best possible work. Students should think of themselves as being on the same game development team, working on all class projects simultaneously. This emphasis on collaboration and cooperation helps students deliver their best work.

Game design classes are focused on students creating practical work that they can put up on a portfolio site to help them get a job in their field. There is certainly a place for game studies courses in which students analyze games, critique them, and consider their place in society. But our focus is on practicing the craft of design.

No one learns how to design games or write for them simply by studying them. You can certainly pick up some pointers and spot things to do (or avoid doing) in your own work, but people learn by doing. Students need opportunities to create their own work, whether it's a prototype of an analog or digital game or the pre-production documents that set the foundation of a game yet to come. All of this work, after further revision and polish, can be placed onto a student's portfolio site to showcase their creative skills.

The ideas presented here should help other instructors convey the design information students need. Current narrative and game designers can use these exercises to develop their skills further, while those hoping to break into the game industry can use these materials to build a stronger portfolio to help launch their careers.

When I teach, I like to include stories from my game industry experiences to illuminate how each succeeding assignment fits into the design process. I try to help students see the relevance of each assignment, each step in the design process as we march toward our end goal (see the "R" in SMART below).

Even if you've never worked in the game industry, it's important to find personal tales you can tell to help make the coursework relevant to your students. Talking about your experiences playing and/or making games and relating those to the content under discussion is crucial to bring home the relevance of that content.

The primary guiding principles of my teaching process are SMART goal-setting and Backward Design. These terms may be familiar to those of you in the education or training fields, but let's take a closer look at how they relate to the teaching of game design and narrative design.

SMART GOAL-SETTING

George T. Doran first proposed the SMART system of goal-setting in the November 1981 issue of *Management Review*.[1] SMART stands for Specific, Measurable, Achievable, Relevant, and Timely. These five elements combine to put any goal within reach. This is especially important in the classroom, as it delivers student achievement and satisfaction with the course content and their mastery of it. Instructors should think of this acronym when designing classes, creating their content, and building the steps along the path to the course's end goal.

Courtesy of Wikimedia Commons. https://commons.wikimedia.org/wiki/
File:SMART-goals.png

Specific reminds instructors to ensure that every task assigned to students is limited in scope, based on your assessment of students' abilities and the time they will have to tackle the work. Try to make the assignment instructions as clear and complete as you can. Both the instructions and scope should be adjusted as you get feedback from students about the difficulties they are having with the assignment.

---

[1] Doran, G. T. (1981). "There's a S.M.A.R.T. way to write management's goals and objectives". *Management Review.* **70** (11): 35–36.

Measurable goals help teachers gauge students' success at each assignment. For many assignments in my design classes, this is very subjective. The creativity a student puts into a concept doc, for example, is a judgment call. The game prototype that a student has created by the end of a class is evaluated on how enjoyable, challenging, or engaging it is. Again, a judgment call. Despite the subjective nature of these assessments, instructors must rely on their own game-creation and teaching experiences to judge these student efforts as fairly and consistently as they can.

Achievable (or *Attainable*) means that the assigned task can be completed by virtually all students within the time limit given. This parameter links with both the Specific and Timely elements to ensure that the assignment is geared toward the knowledge and skill levels of students in the class. Making an assignment achievable is intended to increase student confidence in their growing mastery of the class content.

Relevant was touched on above, but instructors should let students know the intended purpose of every week's content and task. This element of SMART goal-setting closely relates to the instructional methodology of Backward Design (discussed below). Every assignment should have a distinct place in the march toward the course's end goal. It's on the instructor to make sure students know why they are being asked to undertake an assignment. Engagement and satisfaction with a course increase when students know the purpose of each assignment and that they are building toward an interesting final product.

Timely (also called *Time-Based*) is probably the most straightforward element of goal-setting. Deciding how long students will have for an assignment and establishing a deadline for it should not be too difficult. Almost all the tasks I assign in my classes have a one-week deadline. With a new assignment, you should do your best to judge how long it will take most students to complete the task. Seeing how they do allows you to make any needed adjustments to the task's scope or desired quality level.

All five SMART parameters work together to ensure the suitability of a task to the audience (the students in your classroom). I've added a number of assignments to a class only to later discover that one or more of the aspects of SMART had not been implemented correctly. For example, when I first had students in my introductory narrative design class create a Game Design Document (GDD) from an earlier concept document, I gave them only a week to complete the task. When I asked students for feedback midway through the semester, the difficulty of completing that task in a week was a common theme. After that, I split the narrative design class's GDD into two parts, with a week to complete each part. Not only is this task now more achievable for students, they also end up with a much better, more thoughtfully completed GDD.

BACKWARD DESIGN

Another suggestion for those looking to build a course in narrative design or game design is to employ a methodology called Backward Design (also known as Understanding by Design), popularized by Jay McTighe and Grant Wiggins in 1998. This process has instructors start at the end—envision the end result of your course (what you want students to take away from it) and work backward from there, all the way to the first day of class.

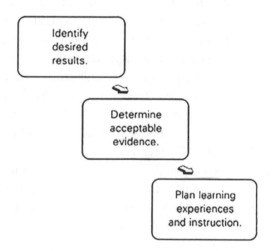

Courtesy of Wikipedia. https://en.wikipedia.org/wiki/Backward_design

For a course in game design, whether analog design or digital, I want students to end up with a working prototype of a game. I also want them to experience as much of the game development process as possible in a classroom setting. For a course in narrative design, I want students to gain as much experience in the narrative designer's actual tasks as possible. I focus primarily on the writing-related tasks that occur during pre-production, as this work concentrates on building the narrative designer's writing and design skills. (Many of the narrative designer's tasks during production depend on interactions with other disciplines on the team, which is hard to simulate in a classroom.)

BACKWARD DESIGN FOR A NARRATIVE DESIGN CLASS

The end result of a narrative design class should be a portfolio of work that spans the gamut of a narrative designer's responsibilities during a video game's pre-production and beyond. The centerpiece of this portfolio is a GDD that serves as the foundation for all the ancillary documents students will complete.

As you can see in the Narrative Design I syllabus in Appendix B, with the above end result in mind, students begin by creating three concept documents. These serve as the starting points for the game design and narrative work to follow. Each concept doc proposes a certain type of game—entertainment, serious/educational, or game adaptation. This gives students a range of concepts to choose from to develop the rest of their work. In my game industry career, I've worked on games that fall into all three categories. It's useful for students to create these documents even in categories that don't initially interest them; you never know when a great idea will come to you in an unexpected venue.

These three types of concept docs are built from templates I provide in Appendix C. For now, suffice it to say that starting from one of these concepts, each student then builds a GDD, expanding upon the basic ideas outlined in that concept doc. Every narrative task to follow builds upon this student's GDD (see the GDD template also in Appendix C).

Over the next ten weeks of the class, every subsequent assignment involves further development of the foundation laid down by the GDD. These are listed in the narrative design class syllabus in Appendix B. For example, students will write short stories set in the game world they are creating—one about the game's hero before the events of the game, another featuring the game's antagonist (the hero's nemesis) as the protagonist, and the third focusing on a character of the student's choice. All three stories serve to further develop the game's story and characters as they were initially presented in the GDD's Story section.

The other tasks that students undertake in my narrative design class build a folio of documents that will complement the GDD, which lays out the core of the game. I also alternate fiction-writing tasks with design-oriented tasks to keep students focused on both these elements of a narrative designer's job. After the first pass at the GDD has been completed, students take the Story section of that document and build upon the initial ideas they described there. They further develop the plot of their game's story, and they expand the cast of characters and develop each of them more, giving them backstories, personalities, and motivations. This requires them to think about how the player will experience their game's story and to work on enhancing its engagement.

Later tasks include writing the opening and ending cinematic scripts for their game to bookend the player's story. Students also write three quest documents that highlight gameplay central to their player experience. These tasks are interspersed with the short story-writing assignments mentioned earlier to alternate fiction writing and game design in the course. These assignments are all listed, with instructions, in Appendix C.

One class each week is devoted to small-group workshops. These give students time to review each other's work, help each other with constructive feedback, and learn from one another's creative efforts. This is a vital element in the learning experience, as students can learn at least as much from each other as from any instructor. Prior to each workshop, I distribute feedback sheets for students to use as guidelines when reviewing and commenting on each other's work.

The final assignment in my narrative design class is for students to take all the work they've done, assemble it into a comprehensive GDD, and then revise all of their work. They leave the class with multiple pieces for a writing and design portfolio—concept docs, a GDD, short stories set in their game world, cinematic scripts, and quest docs. I urge students to continue revising each of these documents and refine them even further for potential employers.

BACKWARD DESIGN FOR A GAME DESIGN CLASS

As with narrative design classes, I use SMART and Backward Design to organize my game design classes. For these classes, the desired end product is a game prototype (sometimes called an MVP—Minimal Viable Product). Each student or group of students should create a prototype that showcases their particular skillset and can impress game industry employers.

The early work in my game design classes follows the same process outlined for narrative design classes. All game work starts with an idea that should be written down into an organized concept document. That leads to a GDD, just as in the narrative classes. But instead of delving into short stories, cinematic scripts, quest docs, and other aspects of a game's story, students in game design classes concentrate on developing gameplay elements.

I teach classes in game design for both analog and digital games. The concept and GDD stages in each class are very similar, with the GDD for digital games requiring students to consider a few more elements, such as the user interface, music and sound. It makes sense that the pre-production stage of these classes, which ends when students' GDDs have been reviewed and revised, is very similar, because at their cores analog and digital games have much the same design; only the implementation differs.

In analog game design classes, students begin implementing their GDD plans as soon as pre-production ends. They bring in their board games, card games, and simple RPGs for playtesting after a week of development. These initial prototypes are very crude, with game design plans only partially implemented, but every game needs to have something for peers to playtest and give feedback on. Students spend the rest of the semester playtesting during class time and working on their games outside of class. This gives each student a game prototype that has undergone multiple playtesting and revision passes, resulting in a well-developed game (including the concept doc and GDD that led to that game).

For digital game design classes, while students are formulating their plans during pre-production, they should also familiarize themselves with the application in which they'll build their game. Students can use a plethora of applications such as Bitsy, RPGMaker, GameMaker Studio, Unity, and Unreal to build their games. To hit the ground running with development once pre-production ends, each student needs to be familiar with at least the basics of the application. As they begin to implement their design at the end of pre-production, their confidence in the application grows rapidly.

Another difference in digital design: Students often do much better when placed on small teams. Analog games are a much lighter load for a single student to handle. But digital games require so many micro-skills (game design, narrative design, sound design, animation, rigging, lighting, art, and so on) that enabling students to share the burden and bring their diverse talents to the project is more likely to set them up for success. To help place students on balanced teams with a good mix of skillsets, instructors should take a survey of student skills across the class early in the semester. Collaborative projects give students a great feel for how they handle teamwork in the game industry.

Whenever I participated in interviews of job candidates at game companies, I always asked about the candidates' collaborative experiences, what issues arose, and how those problems were solved. Working on teams and experiencing the interplay between creativity and teamwork is vital experience for anyone who wants to work in the game industry. When students get that collaboration in the classroom, it gives them a leg up on others to be able to recount those experiences and what they learned from them.

FEEDBACK

All my classes integrate various forms of peer feedback for students. Face-to-face feedback sessions are the most valuable, but even peer reviews parceled out by your school's digital Learning Management System (Canvas, Blackboard, Moodle, etc.) can provide students with helpful advice. The experience of thinking about someone else's work, telling them what's good about it and what could be improved, and getting the same feedback on your work is invaluable preparation for feedback sessions in the game industry.

It's vital to use class time to get students into small feedback groups to review each other's work. The process of thinking about the work someone else did and coming up with commentary on it can not only help the author improve their work, but it also helps the reviewer by exposing them to others' ideas and creativity. Many students have discovered that they can incorporate others' ideas into their own work to improve it. Borrowing ideas from others is a time-honored tradition in the game industry, so it should be fair game in design classes as well.

Feedback isn't just pointing out the negatives in someone's work. Students (and teachers) should point out the positives: What you like about that person's writing, design, or game. Reinforce the work's high points even as you try to help lift the low ones.

The feedback process isn't just for students. Instructors can use feedback from students to help improve their classes, both for current and future students. Midway through each semester, I spend some time getting comments from students about how the class is going. I base this on a process I learned in the game industry called "Stop, Start, Continue."

The gist is that you make lists of what you're doing that's going well in the class (Continue), what's going badly (Stop), and what you aren't doing but maybe should be (Start). Students supply the entries under these categories, with the instructor prompting them to say what's working, what isn't, and what might work instead. Writing these lists down on the whiteboard as students call out entries makes for a fun and informative classroom activity. It gives students a stake in the way the class is run and helps them feel in charge of their learning experience. And it gives the instructor feedback from the people who are most intimately acquainted with the class—the students who are experiencing it.

I find this exercise invaluable. It has improved every class I've taught. You can find and fix processes that aren't working immediately, and improve the experience for both current students and future ones. As long as changes are emailed to all students in the class, they can be made to classes on the fly with instant effect. Students greatly appreciate this flexibility on the part of instructors as well as their willingness to take feedback on their classes.

At the end of each semester, most universities ask students to fill out anonymous, end-of-course evaluations. These can be valuable for learning a few new things about students' impressions of your class and teaching style, but I always want to know more. The final assignment in my classes is a Reflection paper (see Appendix C). In it, I ask students to give me their feelings about the class, what went well and what didn't, what they liked best about the class, and what they liked the least. I tell students this isn't an opportunity for flattery but instead a chance to give honest, helpful feedback that will make the class better for future students.

The final meeting of each class in a semester is a course wrap-up session in which we discuss the learning objectives of the course. I ask if students feel those have been met. If any weren't met, I ask what we might have done differently. This feedback is invaluable in planning the next iteration of the class. I've always gotten at least a couple of good ideas for new things to try. Again, students appreciate being asked for their opinions. Listening to their ideas ends the course on a good note for everyone.

I hope the preceding advice helps others develop game design and narrative design courses for their students. Much of the content and progression of these courses came from my experiences in the game industry, but a good part of my existing coursework has evolved from discussions and experiences with students.

I am always open to advice from others. If you wish to pass along thoughts on these courses or this book, please contact me at michaelbreault@webster.edu.

CHAPTER 13

Career Opportunities in the Game Industry

O NE QUESTION I'VE BEEN asked in every class is how to break into the game industry. Students have widely varying knowledge of what's involved in this process.

When I got into the game industry, back in 1984, there were no college programs for anything related to game design or narrative design. I learned design by doing it. Today there are hundreds of game design programs at universities across the country. But while the opportunity to learn game design in school has vastly expanded, it's harder than ever to break into the industry.

Game development companies overwhelmingly want to hire industry veterans. There are several reasons for this. One is that game development is very much a craft, an occupation learned by doing. When a company compares an industry veteran to someone coming out of college, the scales are weighed heavily in favor of the veteran. That person has demonstrated by their career longevity that they can get along with others on a project. They can channel their creativity to dovetail with that of others and collaborate on a game. And they've shown that they can tough it out through the rough spots that every game development process hits. They have the soft skills game companies want.

Veterans have honed their craft in the years they've been in the industry. They've learned the tricks of their trade by working alongside others with years of experience. It's learning by doing enhanced by mentoring from more-experienced developers.

Most recent college grads have none of the above advantages. They don't have much proof that they can work well within a large, collaborative environment. They don't have the experience of daily mentoring that industry veterans have had. And whether they can channel their creativity in a direction that benefits the team is an open question. Those are huge disadvantages when compared to industry veterans, at least in the minds of interviewers. A prospective employee's collaborative experiences are always of interest to game companies.

Students fresh from game design programs usually won't have real experience on professional development teams, but instructors can give them simulations of those experiences by incorporating group projects into classes. While this doesn't substitute for actual experience in a professional environment, it does help alleviate concerns about how well a new grad will work with others on a team.

CONNECTIONS

In the game industry, who you know gives you the chance to show what you know. Your connections in the industry are crucial to hearing about upcoming job listings and getting a leg up on interview invitations. But those connections just help you get your foot in the door; they don't give you jobs. Getting a job in the game industry requires you to have the skills and personality needed for that position. And that's totally on you.

So, how do you make those connections? Rarely at conventions and conferences, in my experience. A contact you make at a conference is sometimes about as deep a connection as opening your front door to see an evangelist with a religious tract standing there. Unless you can stand out in a very big crowd, your contact with a recruiter is likely to be immediately forgotten.

Real connections, the ones that can help you in your career, are formed by working with people. Only those who have worked with you on a project can vouch for you as a teammate. They can act as true references and tell someone honestly what you're like as a co-worker. And they also know whether they'd like to work with you again or not.

Connections have helped me greatly in my career. I started out at TSR (the *Dungeons & Dragons*® game folks) in 1984 and worked there for five years, plus another three as a freelancer after leaving. Two people I worked with back then were at Zenimax Online Studios (the company that made the *Elder Scrolls Online* MMO) when I interviewed there in 2012, almost 30 years later. I was hired at ZOS partly because those two former co-workers remembered me as a good teammate. When I was hired as a fulltime narrative designer at Volition (the company that made the *Red Faction* and *Saints Row* series, among other games) in 1999, the VP of Development was someone I'd worked with five years earlier as a free-lancer, and he remembered liking my work. There have also been several instances in which I've helped former co-workers get jobs at companies I was working for, solely because I enjoyed working with them the first time and wanted to work with them again.

Students should start building their network of connections in college. Their professors should be part of their network, as long as students do good work in their classes and interact with them. It's easy to do this: Just participate in classroom discussions, talk to the professor outside of class, and take advantage of their office hours. Make yourself known to them as someone interesting, engaged, and who does good work.

College is also where students make strong connections with peers through game projects and clubs. Fellow students can be a tremendous boost to your career—as you each enter the game industry, you can help each other with recommendations as jobs become available at your com-panies. But you have to establish those relationships during your college years to add those peers to your connections network.

BREAKING INTO THE GAME INDUSTRY

As you likely know, breaking into the game industry can be a time-consuming and discouraging undertaking. It's hard to get a job in this indu-stry without experience, but how do you break in to get that experience?

My strongest suggestion to students about to graduate is to actively seek out positions in QA (Quality Assurance—the people who playtest games professionally for game companies). When you look at game industry job boards, such as the ones at https://jobs.gamasutra.com/, one requirement you'll see repeatedly is experience. Posting after posting asks for "three AAA publications" or "five years of professional experience."

QA is the best way to get that experience in my opinion. The require-ments for a QA job are basically that you enjoy playing games, that you play the sorts of games a particular company makes, and that you think about the games you play. Interviewers want QA candidates to be able to talk intelligently about games and to show that they can think analytically about the games they play, noting what works and what could be improved. A very common question in any game industry interview is, "Tell me about a game you've played recently." This is especially important for those seeking QA positions.

Those who haven't been in the game industry may assume QA departments have minimal entry requirements. Nothing could be further from the truth. Most of the QA people I've known have college degrees. But they recognized that QA was their way into the industry and they were willing to put some time in that position while they waited for their chance to step up into a development job.

Many of the developers I've worked with in the game industry have come up from a start in QA positions. I've known programmers, sound designers, game designers, producers, and creative directors who started out as QA. The man who was VP of Development at Volition when I was there, and who later became president of the company, started out in QA. QA might not be a dream job, but it's a great foot in the door. Think of it as an apprenticeship in a field that places much greater value on experience in the industry than in degrees and skills learned in school.

Even though you have a much better chance of getting a QA job than a game developer position when fresh out of college, you should continue to apply for jobs in your field (in addition to QA jobs). This gives you experience in researching companies, crafting cover letters, and filling out applications. In many cases you'll never hear back, but that's par for the course in the game industry. You lose out on 100% of the jobs you don't apply for, so why not apply?

In short, apply for game developer jobs realizing that you're unlikely to get a phone interview, but really pursue QA jobs, as those are much more likely to be your ticket into the game industry.

One experience that can help you land a game industry job is a semester or more of industry internships while still in college. Internships at game companies give you invaluable experience learning your craft from veterans. They can give you a leg up on any fulltime jobs that open up at that company, and they also enable you to build a list of game industry veterans who can attest to your performance on a game project. If possible, talk to your college's internship office to get help in advancing your career.

INDIES VS. AAA

Another question students often ask is whether they should seek opportunities at small indie companies or at larger studios. The answer is simple: If you're fresh out of college, apply for any job in the game industry that you might remotely be a candidate for, no matter how small the company. Experience is what you're looking for at the start of your career, so plan on bootstrapping your way up to the company and position you have your heart set on.

When I talk to my students about their career prospects, I try not to be too pessimistic while at the same time conveying the realities of the situation. Almost all the innovation in the game industry is coming from indie companies. This has been true for several years now and is likely to continue. Students should consider forming their own game companies after graduation with former classmates, even if it is something they must do while working at a day job. Put together a group that you know has the skillsets to conceptualize and develop a game.

When you work with other students on group projects during college, you end up finding people you work well with, who complement your skillset with their own. If you're a game designer, teaming up with a programmer and an artist gives you a great foundation for the start of an indie company. You just need some support from your university, family, or community to start making this a reality.

In your own indie company, each member will need to wear more hats and stretch to learn new skillsets that others in the group don't currently have. It's also a great opportunity: Taking on the responsibilities of a game design lead, a producer, or a creative director is an opportunity that wouldn't come for five or ten years at most established game companies.

During my decades in the game industry, I noticed that the people I worked with who'd been with a company for 20 years or more were all present at the company's founding or soon thereafter. The indie company you form with a few friends from college may turn out to be your lifelong employer. Keep that in the back of your mind as you're working at your little company and looking for work at industry giants.

While innovation may be lacking at many large studios, they are more stable than most indies or student-founded companies. There are no guarantees even then, as you likely know. I joined a company called 38 Studios about five years into their efforts to create an innovative MMO. Nine months later the company ran out of money and folded very suddenly, throwing all employees out of work. When the *Elder Scrolls Online* was released by Zenimax, it greatly underperformed (for reasons mentioned in an earlier chapter). The company suffered through three rounds of layoffs in the months following release; I was caught in the third one.

Sometimes events from well beyond the game industry can affect your job. When I was at Raven Software, we were working on a James Bond game that was to be released when the second Bond movie with Daniel Craig came out. But the movie's publisher, MGM Studios, went bankrupt, the movie was delayed, and our project was canceled. Sensing that a lay-off was in the wind, I quickly found a job at Ubisoft Montreal and gave Raven two weeks' notice. On my last day at Raven, they announced a layoff affecting 30–40 developers at the studio.

There are no sure bets in the game industry. But I've made a 35-year career out of it, and I know many others who have as well. It requires persistence, a belief in oneself and one's talent, and the ability to weather adversity. I've found it to be a very rewarding career, and I hope you do as well.

Courtesy of NeedPix.com.

Appendix A

Publications List

For anyone who might be interested, this appendix lists the more than 130 products I have worked on in the course of my 35-year career in the game industry. An electronic version of this list can be found by searching for my name under Designers on the *boardgamegeek.com* website's search function.

COMPUTER AND VIDEO GAMES

- *Elder Scrolls Online: Imperial City*, Zenimax, 2015 (narrative design and scripting)

- *Elder Scrolls Online*, Zenimax, 2014 (narrative design and scripting)

- *Project Copernicus*, 38 Studios, unpublished, 2012 (narrative design)

- *Far Cry 3*, Ubisoft Montreal, 2011 (narrative design)

- *Project Legend*, Ubisoft Montreal, unpublished, 2010 (narrative design)

- *Call of Duty: Black Ops*, Activision, 2010 (scripting)

- *Singularity*, Raven Software, 2010 (narrative design)

- *Project James Bond*, Raven Software, unpublished, 2010 (narrative design)

- *Wolfenstein*, Raven Software, 2009 (game design and narrative design)

- *Red Faction: Guerrilla*, Volition, 2008 (game design and narrative design)

- *Saints Row*, Volition, 2008 (narrative design)

- *The Punisher*, Volition, 2005 (game design and narrative design)

- *Red Faction 2*, Volition, 2002 (game design and scripting)

- *Summoner 2*, Volition, 2002 (narrative design)

- *Red Faction*, Volition, 2001 (game design, narrative design, and scripting)

- *Summoner*, Volition, 2000 (narrative design)

- *Freespace 2*, Volition, 1999 (narrative design)

- *West Point Atlas of Wars*, Digital Impact, unpublished, 1998 (game design and narrative design)

- *Ozzie's Science World*, Educational Insights, 1997 (game design and narrative design)

- *Top Gun: Fire at Will!*, Spectrum Holobyte, 1996 (game design and narrative design)

- *Where in the World is Carmen Sandiego*, Bröderbund, 1995 (manual writing)

- *The Voyages of Magellan*, VTech, unpublished, 1995 (game design and narrative design)

- *King Arthur and the Knights of Justice*, Enix America, 1994 (narrative design)

- *SSN-21 Seawolf*, Electronic Arts, 1994 (game design and narrative design)

- *Inherit the Earth: Quest for the Orb*, The Dreamers Guild, 1994 (game design)

- *Zurk's Learning Safari*, Soleil Software, 1993 (testing)

- *Hunters of Ralk*, Cyberdreams, unpublished, 1993 (game design and narrative design)

- *Shining Force II*, Sega, 1993 (narrative design)

- *Jeopardy!*, Gametek, 1993 (game design and narrative design)

- *Dungeons and Dragons: Warriors of the Eternal Sun*, Sega, 1992 (narrative design)

- *Home Alone 2*, Capstone, 1992 (narrative design)

- *Day Dreamin' Davey*, HAL America, 1992 (narrative design)

- *Shining Force*, Sega, 1992 (narrative design)

- *Castles: The Northern Campaign*, Interplay, 1991 (game design and narrative design)

- *Shining in the Darkness*, Sega, 1991 (narrative design)

- *Robin Hood: Prince of Thieves*, Virgin Games, 1991 (game design and narrative design)

- *Phantasy Star III*, Sega, 1990 (narrative design)

- *Sword of Vermilion*, Sega, 1989 (narrative design)

- *Pool of Radiance*, SSI, 1988 (game design and narrative design)

COMPUTER GAME STRATEGY GUIDES

- *Apocalypse*, BradyGames, 1998 (editing and development)

- *Heretic II*, BradyGames, 1998 (editing and development)

- *Klingon Honor Guard*, BradyGames, 1998 (editing and development)

- *Lego Creator*, BradyGames, 1998 (editing and development)

- *Small Soldiers*, BradyGames, 1998 (editing and development)

- *Trespasser*, BradyGames, 1998 (editing and development)

- *Vigilance*, BradyGames, 1998 (editing and development)

- *Dungeons & Dragons: Warriors of the Eternal Sun*, SSI, 1992 (writing)

- *Phantasy Star III*, Sega of America, 1991 (writing)

BOARD GAMES

- *God's Demon,* currently under development (design and writing)

- *HeroQuest: Barbarian Quest Pack*, Milton Bradley, 1992 (editing and development)

- *HeroQuest: Elf Quest Pack*, Milton Bradley, 1992 (editing and development)

- *HeroQuest: Dwarf Quest Pack*, Milton Bradley, unpublished (editing and development)

- *HeroQuest: Wizard Quest Pack*, Milton Bradley, unpublished (editing and development)

- *World War II: Pacific Theater of Operations*, SPI, 1991 (editing and development)

- *Crosse*, TSR, 1988 (editing and development)

- *I Think You Think I Think*, TSR, 1988 (writing, editing, and development)

- *Kage*, TSR, 1988 (editing and development)

- *Steppe*, TSR, 1988 (editing and development)

- *Gammarauders*, TSR, 1987 (editing and development)

- *Chase*, TSR, 1986 (editing and development)

PAPER ROLE-PLAYING GAMES

- *Dragonlance Classics: 15th Anniversary Pack*, Advanced Dungeons and Dragons, TSR, 1999 (editing and development)

- *Dragonlance Classics: Volume III*, AD&D, TSR, 1994 (editing and development)

- *Code of the Harpers*, AD&D, TSR, 1993 (editing and development)

- *Dragonlance: New Tales*, AD&D, TSR, 1993 (editing and development)

- *Al-Qadim: City of Delights*, AD&D 2nd Edition boxed set, TSR, 1993 (editing and development)

- *The Glory of Rome*, AD&D 2nd Edition, TSR, 1993 (editing and development)

- *Charlemagne's Paladins*, AD&D 2nd Edition, TSR, 1992 (editing and development)

- *The Complete Bard's Handbook*, AD&D 2nd Edition, TSR, 1992 (editing and development)

- *Ravenloft: Forbidden Lore*, AD&D 2nd Edition boxed set, TSR, 1992 (editing and development)

- *Dragonlance: Flint's Axe*, AD&D, TSR, 1992 (editing and development)

- *Dark Sun: Dune Trader*, AD&D, TSR, 1992 (editing and development)

- *Dark Sun: Slave Tribes*, AD&D, TSR, 1992 (editing and development)

- *Dragonlance: Wild Elves*, AD&D, TSR, 1991 (editing and development)

- *Greyhawk: Howl from the North*, AD&D, TSR, 1991 (editing and development)

- *Prince of Lankhmar*, AD&D, TSR, 1991 (editing and development)

- *Ravenloft: Darklords*, AD&D, TSR, 1991 (editing and development)

- *Ravenloft: Ship of Horror*, AD&D, TSR, 1991 (editing and development)

- *Monstrous Compendium: Volume 2*, AD&D 2nd Edition, TSR, 1990 (editing and development)

- *Monstrous Compendium: Volume 3*, AD&D 2nd Edition, TSR, 1990 (editing and development)

- *Monstrous Compendium: Spelljammer*, AD&D 2nd Edition, TSR, 1990 (editing and development)

- *Monstrous Compendium: Greyhawk*, AD&D 2nd Edition, TSR, 1990 (editing and development)

- *Draconomicon*, AD&D, TSR, 1990 (editing and development)

- *Dragonlance: Dragon Knight*, AD&D, TSR, 1990 (editing and development)

- *Dragonlance: Dragon's Rest*, AD&D, TSR, 1990 (editing and development)

- *Dragonlance: Otherlands*, AD&D, TSR, 1990 (editing and development)

- *Greyhawk: Flames of the Falcon*, AD&D, TSR, 1990 (editing and development)

- *Greyhawk: Vecna Lives!*, AD&D, TSR, 1990 (editing and development)

- *Old Empires*, AD&D, TSR, 1990 (editing and development)

- *Dragonlance Classics: Volume I*, AD&D, TSR, 1990 (editing and development)

- *Monstrous Compendium*, AD&D 2nd Edition, TSR, 1989 (editing and development)

- *Greyhawk Adventures: City of Greyhawk*, AD&D 2nd Edition, boxed set, TSR, 1989 (editing and development)

- *Dungeon Master's Guide*, AD&D 2nd Edition hardback book, TSR, 1989 (editing and development)

- *Player's Handbook*, AD&D 2nd Edition hardback book, TSR, 1989 (editing and development)

- *Time of the Dragon*, AD&D 2nd Edition boxed set, TSR, 1989 (editing and development)

- *Ruins of Adventure*, AD&D, TSR, 1989 (writing, editing, and development)

- *Dragonlance: Dragon Keep*, AD&D, TSR, 1989 (editing and development)

- *Dragonlance: In Search of Dragons*, AD&D, TSR, 1989 (editing and development)

- *Greyhawk: Vale of the Mage*, AD&D, TSR, 1989 (editing and development)

- *Dragonlance: The World of Krynn*, AD&D, TSR, 1988 (editing and development)

- *Dragonlance: The Mists of Krynn*, AD&D, TSR, 1988 (editing and development)

- *Greyhawk: Castle Greyhawk*, AD&D, TSR, 1988 (editing and development)

- *Throne of Bloodstone*, AD&D, TSR, 1988 (editing and development)

- *Dragonlance Adventures*, AD&D hardback book, TSR, 1987 (editing and development)

- *Manual of the Planes*, AD&D hardback book, TSR, 1987 (editing and development)

- *Moonshae*, AD&D, TSR, 1987 (editing and development)

- *Ochimo: The Spirit Warrior*, AD&D, TSR, 1987 (editing and development)

- *Dungeoneer's Survival Guide*, AD&D, TSR, 1986 (editing and development)

- *Dragonlance: Dragons of Triumph*, AD&D, TSR, 1986 (editing and development)

- *Dragonlance: Dragons of Truth*, AD&D, TSR, 1986 (editing and development)

- *Dragonlance: Dragons of Faith*, AD&D, TSR, 1986 (editing and development)

- *The Mines of Bloodstone*, AD&D, TSR, 1986 (editing and development)

- *Swords of the Daimyo*, AD&D, TSR, 1986 (editing and development)

- *The Book of Lairs*, AD&D, TSR, 1986 (writing, editing, and development)

- *Oriental Adventures*, AD&D hardback book, TSR, 1985 (editing and development)

- *Dragonlance: Dragons of Glory*, AD&D, TSR, 1985 (editing and development)

- *Dragonlance: Dragons of Deceit*, AD&D, TSR, 1985 (editing and development)

- *Dragonlance: Dragons of War*, AD&D, TSR, 1985 (editing and development)

- *Dragonlance: Dragons of Light*, AD&D, TSR, 1985 (editing and development)

- *Dragonlance: Dragons of Ice*, AD&D, TSR, 1985 (editing and development)

- *The Golden Khan of Ethengar*, D&D, TSR, 1989 (editing and development)

- *Crown of Ancient Glory*, D&D, TSR, 1987 (editing and development)

- *Wrath of Olympus,* D&D, TSR, 1987 (editing and development)
- *Creature Catalogue,* D&D, TSR, 1986 (editing and development)
- *Gamer's Handbook of the Marvel Universe,* Marvel Super Heroes, TSR, 1991 (editing and development)
- *After Midnight,* Marvel Super Heroes, TSR, 1990 (editing and development)
- *Cosmos Cubed,* Marvel Super Heroes, TSR, 1988 (editing and development)
- *The X- Potential,* Marvel Super Heroes, TSR, 1987 (editing and development)
- *Gamma World,* 3rd Edition boxed set, TSR, 1988 (editing and development)
- *Zebulon's Guide to Frontier Space,* Star Frontiers, TSR, 1985 (editing and development)
- *Face of the Enemy,* Star Frontiers, TSR, 1984 (editing and development)
- *The Belt,* Buck Rogers, TSR, 1991 (editing and development)
- *Inner Worlds,* Buck Rogers, TSR, 1991 (editing and development)
- *A Matter of Gravitol,* Buck Rogers, TSR, 1991 (editing and development)
- *Buck Rogers: Play-by-Mail Game,* Buck Rogers, TSR, 1990 (editing and development)
- *Buck Rogers in the 25th Century,* Buck Rogers, TSR, 1990 (editing and development)
- *Covert Operations Source Book, Volume 2,* Top Secret, TSR, 1988 (editing)
- *Covert Operations Source Book,* Top Secret, TSR, 1987 (editing and development)
- *Conan Role-Playing Game,* boxed set, Conan, TSR, 1984 (editing and development)
- *Lazer Tag Official Game Handbook,* TSR, 1987 (editing and development)

Appendix B

Class Syllabi

The following syllabi show the progression of content in each type of class that I teach. They provide a week-by-week summary of the learning content delivered to students. All instructions and templates for the assignments (quests) listed below can be found in Appendix C. These are included both to help instructors review potential content for their game design and narrative design classes and to give students and industry practitioners ideas for work to undertake to improve their design and writing skills.

NARRATIVE DESIGN I SYLLABUS

Overview

This course focuses on practical aspects of writing for digital games, including but not limited to story structure, character creation, dialogue, theme, cinematics, the interactive nature of the medium, and the intersections of story and gameplay. Students analyze narrative and the writing process to better understand the unique challenges of digital game narrative. Students also apply principles of game design, development, and production to the narrative process. Students are expected to improve the quality of their writing as well as their understanding of narrative structures for digital games.

Course Learning Outcomes

- To improve students' writing, thinking, and cooperative feedback skills.

- To familiarize students with the role of a narrative designer in the game industry.

- To demonstrate the complex interactions between story and design in games.

- To help interested students develop a narrative design and game design portfolio.

Materials

- There is no required textbook for this course.

- Recommended: Lee Sheldon, *Character Development and Storytelling for Games*, 2nd Edition, Cengage.

- Internet articles and videos will be utilized as needed.

Week 1—Introductions, Story Thoughts

- Tues: Introductions, Class Goals and Setup, Syllabus.

- Thurs: Discussion: Concept documents.

  - Quest 1: Concept doc, 1 page (entertainment, template provided).

  - Optional Reading: *Sheldon*, Part I: Background, Ch. 1, Ch. 2.

Week 2—Concept Docs, Plot vs. Story

- Tues: Discussion: Plot vs. Story, arcade game short story assignment.

- Thurs: Workshop: Concept docs (Q1).

  - Quest 2: Arcade game short story.

  - Optional Reading: Student examples of arcade game short stories.

Week 3—Games and Players, Serious Games

- Tues: Game design and players. Writing, serious/educational games.

- Thurs: Workshop: Arcade Stories (Q2).

  - Quest 3: Serious concept doc, 1 page (template).

  - Reading: Student examples of serious/educational concept docs.

Week 4—Game Adaptations

- Tues: Discussion: Game adaptations; game genres and players.

- Thurs: Workshop: Serious Concepts (Q3).

- Quest 4: Game adaptation concept doc, 1 page (template).
- Reading: Student examples of game adaptation concept docs.

Week 5—GDDs

- Tues: Discussion: Concept to design, Game Design Document (GDDs), story and characters.
- Thurs: Workshop: Game Adaptation Concepts (Q4).
  - Quest 5: GDD, Part 1 (template).
  - Reading: Sample GDDs from previous classes.

Week 6—Stories in Games

- Tues: Discussion: Stories in games.
- Thurs: Workshop: GDD, Part 1 (Q5).
  - Quest 6: Short story set in your game world.
  - Reading: Sample short stories from previous classes.

Week 7—GDDs Redux

- Tues: GDD issues, weaknesses.
- Thurs: Workshop: Short Stories (Q6).
  - Quest 7: GDD, Part 2.
  - Reading: Sample GDDs from previous classes.

Week 8—Integrating Story and Gameplay

- Tues: Discussion: Integrating story with gameplay.
- Thurs: Workshop: Complete GDDs (Parts 1 and 2) (Q7).
  - Quest 8: Write a two- to four-page paper about the integration of story with gameplay in a published video game.
  - Reading: Sample story/gameplay integration papers from previous classes.

Week 9—The Hero's Journey

- Tues: Discussion: GDD issues. Hero's Journey. Story and characters in games.

- Thurs: Workshop: Story-gameplay integration papers (Q8).

  - Quest 9: Develop the Story section of GDD more fully, populate with characters, and explore motivations, roles, and relationships.

  - Reading: Sample story section revisions from previous classes.

Week 10—Cinematics

- Tues: Discussion: Cinematics, starting and ending games.

- Thurs: Workshop: Story section of GDD (Q9).

  - Quest 10: Write your game's opening and ending cinematic scripts.

  - Reading: Sample cinematic scripts from previous classes.

Week 11—The Hero and the Shadow

- Tues: Discussion: The Hero and the Shadow—driving your game's story.

- Thurs: Workshop: Cinematic scripts (Q10).

  - Quest 11: Write a two- to four-page short story about your game's Shadow.

  - Reading: Sample Shadow stories from previous classes.

Week 12—Quests

- Tues: Discussion: Story-based quests, integrating story with gameplay.

- Thurs: Workshop: Shadow stories (Q11).

  - Quest 12: Develop three quests/missions that complement your game's story and highlight gameplay.

  - Reading: Sample quests from previous classes.

Week 13—Stories and Quests

- Tues: Discussion: The revision process.

- Thurs: Workshop: Quests (Q12).

Week 14—Rewriting and Revision

- Tues: Discussion: Revisit short story discussion, fiction set in game worlds.

- Thurs: Workshop: Bring in a previous (game-related) short story for revision suggestions.

  - Quest 13A: Write another short story set in your game world, not about the Hero, Shadow, or previous protagonist. OR

  - Quest 13B: Make a major revision to a short story previously written for this class, using feedback received from classmates and instructor.

  - Reading: More student short stories.

Week 15—Course Wrap-Up

- Tues: Workshop: Short stories (Q13).

- Thurs: Final class! Course wrap-up and feedback. Fill out evaluations.

  - Quest 14: Revise and expand upon all elements in GDD.

  - Quest 15: Write a brief Reflection paper about your experiences in this class.

Grade Components (1,000 Points Total)

Attendance and Participation (peer reviews and DBs): 200 points.
  Quests 1–13: 50 points each (650 points total).
  Quest 14: 125 points.
  Quest 15: 25 points.
  TOTAL—1,000 points.

Attendance Policy

Attendance is part of your Participation grade. Miss more than one class and it will lower that grade. How much it lowers your grade depends on the other aspects of your participation—peer reviews, discussion board (DB) participation, playtesting and feedback, and so on.

NARRATIVE DESIGN II SYLLABUS

Overview

This course builds upon the lessons learned in our Narrative Design I course. Students work collaboratively and separately on a variety of narrative design and game design assignments. This course emphasizes engaging writing, but developing creative game design figures prominently as well. Interactive fiction is a focus, with students studying existing IF games and developing one or more of their own (in Twine2 app).

Course Learning Outcomes

- To improve students' writing, thinking, and cooperative feedback skills.

- To familiarize students with the role of a narrative designer in the game industry.

- To familiarize students with the field of interactive fiction/text adventures.

- To demonstrate the complex interactions between story and design in games.

- To help interested students develop a narrative design or game design portfolio.

Materials

- There is no required textbook for this course.

- Recommended: Lee Sheldon, *Character Development and Storytelling for Games*, 2nd Edition, Cengage.

- Internet articles and videos will be utilized as needed.

Week 1—Introductions, Class Goals and Expectations, Syllabus, Concept/ss

- Quest 1: Concept/pitch doc, 1 page (entertainment genre, template provided).

- Readings: Introduction to Twine2:

  - http://www.auntiepixelante.com/twine/

  - https://www.youtube.com/watch?v=5yCZaQLb_Kw&index=1&l
    ist=PLlXuD3kyVEr5tlic4SRe6ZG-R9OyS1T4d

    - At least first (intro) video; look at more if you have time.

Week 2—Discussion: Story. Workshop Reading and Feedback.

- Quest 2: Students in each workgroup trade concepts. Each student writes a story and cast of characters to go with another student's concept doc.

- Workshop: Review and give feedback on each others' concept docs.

- Readings: More Twine2:

  - https://www.youtube.com/watch?v=1jukyU4EK2M&list=PLFgj
    YYTq6xyjBtXJTvEaBTVUWxirY6q24

Week 3—Discussion: Game Design Discussion.
Workshop Reading and Feedback

- Quest 3: Students trade concept and story docs. Each creates a game world/setting doc to go with the other students' concept/story combos.

- Workshop: Review and give feedback on concept/story combos.

- Readings: More Twine2:

  - http://www.gamasutra.com/blogs/DanCox/20130218/186810/
    Learning_Twine_Part_3.php

  - https://www.youtube.com/watch?v=zVKtU0cvb6k

Week 4—Discussion: Cinematics. Workshop Reading and Feedback

- Quest 4: Each student takes the concept/story/setting combo created by the other three students in their workgroup and writes two cinematic scripts to complement that package—an opening cinematic and an ending cinematic.

- Workshop: Review and give feedback on concept/story/setting packages.

- Readings: Continue to study Twine2 videos in links given above.

Week 5—Discussion: Text Adventures, Interactive Fiction. Workshop Reading and Feedback

- Quest 5: Play an IF game from the following list and write a 1–2 page analysis of its story and gameplay. Think about takeaways for the game you will create.

    - Space Suit (http://ifdb.tads.org/viewgame?id=1mfe25emkc3o1eo9).

    - Beneath Floes (https://bravemule.itch.io/beneathfloes).

    - Adventure (http://ifdb.tads.org/viewgame?id=fft6pu91j85y4acv— click "Play Online").

- Workshop: Review entire game design package developed from each concept in group.

- Reading: Assignment counts as this week's reading.

Week 6—Discussion: Game Design. Workshop Reading and Feedback

- Quest 6: Each student develops a GDD (from template aimed at IF games) from the concept they created in this class.

    - Story outline, characters, setting, gameplay elements.

- Workshop: Discuss the IF game each student in group played, review their analysis, discuss lessons to be taken from each game.

- Reading: Continue to study Twine2 videos in links given above.

Week 7—Discussion: The Player Experience. Workshop Reading and Feedback

- Quest 7: Each student flowcharts a plan for how their game will be presented to players, detailing the player's path through the game's story.

    - Suggest flowcharting apps!

- Workshop: Review and give feedback on GDDs.

- Reading: Continue to study Twine2 videos in links given above.

Week 8—Discussion: IF and Text Adventure
Principles. Workshop Reading and Feedback

- Quest 8: Revise and expand GDD according to feedback.

- Workshop: Review and give feedback on flowcharts.

- Reading: Continue to study Twine2 videos in links given above.

Week 9—Discussion: GDD Issues. Workshop Reading and Feedback

- Quest 9: Begin creating game; work in progress. Bring game to class.

- Workshop: Play student games, provide feedback in DBs.

- Reading: Continue to study Twine2 videos in links given above—as needed.

Week 10—Discussion: IF and Text Adventure Game
Issues. Workshop Reading and Feedback

- Quest 10: Continue developing game. Bring game to class.

- Workshop: Play student games, provide feedback in DBs.

- Reading: Continue to study Twine2 videos in links given above—as needed.

Week 11—Discussion: Student Games' Issues.
Workshop Reading and Feedback

- Quest 11: Continue developing game. Bring game to class.

- Workshop: Play student games, provide feedback in DBs.

- Reading: Continue to study Twine2 videos in links given above—as needed.

Week 12—Discussion: Student Games' Issues.
Workshop Reading and Feedback

- Quest 12: Continue developing game. Bring game to class.

- Workshop: Play student games, provide feedback in DBs.

- Reading: Continue to study Twine2 videos in links given above—as needed.

Week 13—Discussion: Student Games' Issues.
Workshop Reading and Feedback

- Quest 13: Continue developing game. Bring game to class.

- Workshop: Play student games, provide feedback in DBs.

- Reading: Continue to study Twine2 videos in links given above—as needed.

Week 14—Discussion: Student Games' Issues.
Workshop Reading and Feedback

- Quest 14: Turn in the final version of game.

Week 15—Discussion: Course and Content Wrapup, Post-Mortem.

- Quest 15: Write a reflection paper about the process to create your game, what worked and what didn't, and what you learned, as well as suggestions for improving the class.

Grade Components (1,000 Points Total)

Attendance and Participation (peer reviews and DBs): 125 points.
    Quests 1–13: 50 points each (650 points total).
    Quest 14: 200 points.
    Quest 15: 25 points.
    TOTAL—1,000 points.

Attendance Policy

Attendance is part of your Participation grade. Miss more than one class and it will lower that grade. How much it lowers your grade depends on the other aspects of your participation—peer reviews, DB participation, playtesting and feedback, and so on.

ANALOG GAME DESIGN SYLLABUS

Overview

In this course, students learn analog game design theory, analyze a variety of board, card, and dice games, and then create their own prototype for the entire class to playtest.

Learning Objectives

- Introduce students to game industry practices and structures.

- Demonstrate in a workshop format the various means of game design and the basic principles of good game design.

- Demonstrate in a workshop format the various means of game development and the basic principles needed for good game development.

- Have students take a game concept, expand upon it in a detailed GDD, then create a prototype that is refined through playtesting.

Outcomes

- Students will understand the analog game industry, both as a hobby and a business.

- Students will gain working knowledge of basic game design principles and practice.

- Students will demonstrate in a workshop format the various means of game development and the basic principles needed for good game development.

- Students will develop a working understanding of how to take an idea through the prototyping and playtesting processes.

Materials

- Recommended but not required:

  - Selinker, Mike. Kobold Guide to Board Game Design (2011).

- Internet videos and articles as needed.

Schedule
Week 1—Starting Up

- Mon: Introduce course, self, go over syllabus—Prezi presentation.

- Weds: Game Design Basics; Game Systems and Game Mechanics.

- Fri: Flow and Progression; Theme in games; player interactions are paramount; Duffer's Drift.

  - Quest 1: Critique the syllabus.

Week 2—Game Design Basics

- Mon:– no class.

- Weds: Play games.

- Fri: Play games.

  - Quest 2: Write analysis of game systems and game mechanics in a game played.

    - Peer Reviews (2) of Quest 2.

Week 3—Players and Genres

- Mon: Game players.

- Weds: Game genres and core systems/mechanics.

- Fri: Definitions of Game Design (3): Player Experience, Journalist's Questions, Honey Badger.

  - Quest 3: Analyze yourself as a gamer, using both Bartle's Taxonomy (for 3+ game genres that you play) and the QF system.

    - Peer Reviews (2).

Week 4—Designing Games

- Mon: The game dev process—pre-development, development, testing, polish.

- Weds: Concept docs.

- Fri: Workshop—Small group brainstorming for concepts.

  - Quest 4: Create two concept docs from the template.

    - Peer Reviews (2).

Week 5—Game Design Docs

- Mon: Workshop—Small groups, read each other's concepts, make suggestions.

- Weds: Talk about GDDs, go over template.
- Fri: Issues, problems with GDDs?
  - Quest 5: GDD, Initial Pass.
    - Peer Reviews (2).

Week 6—GDDs Continued

- Mon: Workshop—Small groups, review GDDs, make suggestions.
- Weds: Workshop—Small groups, review GDDs, make suggestions.
- Fri: Talk about GDD issues. Workshop—Small groups, review GDDs, make suggestions.
  - Quest 6: GDD, Second Pass.
    - Peer Reviews (2).

Week 7—Pre-Production to Development

- Mon: Talk about developing games from GDDs.
- Weds: Workshop—review second-pass GDDs, make suggestions.
- Fri: Workshop—review second-pass GDDs, make suggestions.
  - Quest 7: Initial Prototype (including rules!).
    - No peer reviews.

Week 8—Playtesting, Round 1

- Mon: Discussion; Playtest student games.
- Weds: Playtest student games.
- Fri: Playtest student games.
  - Quest 8: Second iteration of game.
    - Feedback (on DBs, for all games played).

Week 9—Playtesting, Round 2

- Mon: Discussion; Playtest student games.

- Weds: Playtest student games.
- Fri: Playtest student games.
  - Quest 9: Third iteration of game.
    - Feedback (on DBs, for all games played).

Week 10—Playtesting, Round 3

- Mon: Discussion; Playtest student games.
- Weds: Playtest student games.
- Fri: Playtest student games.
  - Quest 10a: Fourth iteration of game. OR
  - Quest 10b: Concept doc and GDD for new game.
    - Feedback (on DBs, all games played).

Week 11—Playtesting, Round 4

- Mon: Discussion; Playtest student games.
- Weds: Playtest student games.
- Fri: Playtest student games.
  - Quest 11a: Fifth iteration of game OR
  - Quest 11b: First iteration of new game.
    - Feedback (on DBs, all games played).

Week 12—Playtesting, Round 5

- Mon: Discussion; Playtest student games.
- Weds: Playtest student games; feedback on games.
- Fri: Playtest student games; feedback on games.
  - Quest 12: Pre-Alpha iteration of game.
    - Feedback (on DBs, all games played).

Week 13—Playtesting, Round 6

- Mon: Discussion; Playtest student games.
- Weds: Playtest student games.
- Fri: Playtest student games.
  - Quest 13: Alpha version of game.
    - Feedback (on DBs, all games played).

Week 14—Playtesting, Round 7

- Mon: Playtest student games.
- Weds: Playtest student games.
- Fri: Playtest student games.
  - Quest 14: Beta version of game.
    - Feedback (on DBs, all games played).

Week 15—Final Playtesting and Course Wrap-Up

- Mon: Playtest student games.
- Weds: Final Playtest of student games.
- Fri: Final class! Course wrap-up and feedback. Fill out evaluations.
  - Feedback (on DBs, all games played).
  - Quest 15: Gold Master (Final) game and rules AND final GDD.
  - Quest 16: Reflection paper.

Grade Components (1,000 Points Total)

Attendance and Participation (including peer reviews): 240 points.
  Quests 1–14: 40 points each (560 points total).
  Quest 15: 150 points.
  Quest 16: 50 points.
  TOTAL—1,000 points possible.

Attendance Policy

Attendance is part of your Participation grade. Miss more than one class and it will lower that grade. How much it lowers it depends on the other aspects of your participation—peer reviews, DB participation, playtesting and feedback, and so on.

WORLD DESIGN SYLLABUS

Overview

This course enables students to explore the principles involved in the development of an expansive game world within an interactive video game. This involves the study of various techniques employed by writers and designers in the development of unique and exciting fictional worlds. Emphasis is placed on conveying the societies and history of your game world.

Learning Outcomes

- Students will gain an increased understanding of the professional requirements for world design in interactive games.

- Students will learn and display techniques employed by writers for film, novels, and games in the development of their world design.

- Students will demonstrate their ability to analyze and incorporate relevant historical and cultural elements into their game world designs.

Materials

- RPGMaker, GameMaker Studio, or Unity.

Schedule

Week 1—Starting Up

- Mon: Introduce course, self, go over syllabus.

  - Quests, Participation (attendance and peer reviews).

  - No test or quizzes.

- Weds: Elements of Game Design; theme (show *Awful Green Things from Outer Space*)

  - Triangle of Weirdness.

- Fri: Talk about game dev environments (RPGMaker, etc.).

Week 2—World Design

- **Mon: LABOR DAY—NO CLASS!**
- Weds: World Design:
  - Setting, story, characters, conflict, action and events.
  - Gives depth and coherence to game world.
  - Answer journalist's questions—WWWWWH?—about your world.
- Fri: Discuss different world designs.
  - Mario Kart, Skyrim; student suggestions.
  - Quest 1: Analysis of world design, game of your choice.
    - Peer Reviews (2).

Week 3—Designing for Players

- Mon: Who are your players? What do they want?
  - Bartle's Taxonomy.
  - Quantic Foundry.
- Weds: Game genres and their players.
- Fri: Tutorials.
  - Quest 2: Analysis of Self as a Gamer (Bartle's and QF).
    - Peer Reviews (2).

Week 4—Concept Docs

- Mon: Concept docs intro, GDDs, and iteration.
- Weds: Aiming concept and GDD at game dev app.
- Fri: Tutorials.
  - Quest 3: Create two concept docs as possible beginnings for your game design.

Week 5—Concept to GDD, Part 1

- Mon: Workshop—small groups read and discuss each other's concepts.

- Weds: Workshop—new groups read and discuss each other's concepts.

- Fri: Tutorials.

  - Quest 4: Develop Part 1 of your GDD from one of your two concepts.

Week 6—GDD, Part 2

- Mon: Workshop—small groups read and discuss each other's GDD, Part 1

- Weds: Workshop—new groups read and discuss each other's GDD, Part 1

- Fri: Tutorials.

  - Quest 5: Develop Part 2 of your GDD.

Week 7—Whole GDD Review and Revision

- Mon: Workshop—small groups review and give feedback on entire GDD.

- Weds: Workshop—new groups review and give feedback on entire GDD.

- Fri: Form teams to work together on a game world.

  - Quest 6: Revise both sections of GDD from feedback.

  - Peer Reviews (2).

Week 8—GDD to Game World

- Mon: Final workshop—GDD revisions, new groups.

- Weds: Work day.

- Fri: Work day.

  - Quest 7: Turn in the initial version of game world.

Week 9—Playtesting, Round 1

- Mon: Playtesting.

  - Feedback (on DBs): Review and give feedback on games played on Monday.

- Weds: Work day.

- Fri: Work day.

  - Quest 8: Turn in Changelog. Revised game due in class.

Week 10—Playtesting, Round 2

- Mon: Work day.

- Weds: Playtesting.

  - Feedback (on DBs): Review and give feedback on games played on Wednesday.

- Fri: Work day.

  - Quest 9: Turn in Changelog. Revised game due in class.

Week 11—Playtesting, Round 3

- Mon: Playtesting.

  - Feedback (on DBs): Review and give feedback on games played on Monday.

- Weds: Work day.

- Fri: Work day.

  - Quest 10: Turn in Changelog. Revised game due in class.

Week 12—Playtesting, Round 4

- Mon: Playtesting.

  - Feedback (on DBs): Review and give feedback on games played on Monday.

- Weds: Work day.

- Fri: Work day.

  - Quest 11: Turn in Changelog. Revised game due in class.

Week 13—Playtesting, Round 5

- Mon: Playtesting.

  - Feedback (on DBs): Review and give feedback on games played on Monday.

- Weds: Work day.

- **Fri: THANKSGIVING BREAK!**

  - Quest 12: Turn in Changelog. Revised game due in class.

Week 14—Playtesting, Final Round

- Mon: Playtesting.

  - Feedback (on DBs): Review and give feedback on games played on Monday.

- Weds: Work day.

- Fri: Work day.

  - Quest 13: Turn in Gold Master (final) version of your game.

Week 15—Wrap-Up

- Mon: Talk about revising GDD to final state. Playtesting games.

- Weds: Discussion. Playtesting games.

- Fri: Final class—wrap-up, feedback, evaluations.

  - Quest 14: Two-part quest – final, revised GDD and Reflection Paper.

Grade Components (1,000 Points Total)

Quest 0 (Attendance and Participation): 150 points.
    Quests 1–12: 50 points each (600 points total).
    Quest 13: 150 points.
    Quest 14: 100 points.
    TOTAL—1,000 points.

Attendance Policy

Attendance is part of your Participation grade. Miss more than one class and it will lower that grade. Be consistently late to class and that will lower your participation grade too. How much it lowers it depends on the other aspects of your participation—peer reviews, DB participation, playtesting and feedback, and so on.

INTRO TO DIGITAL GAME DESIGN SYLLABUS

Overview

This course gives students an overview of video game development. Students learn about game design and other aspects of games and gaming. A strong emphasis of this class is on deconstruction and critique of popular computer and console games and genres. Students undertake a "devolver" project, in which each teams analyze a video game and create an analog game that conveys the original's essential gameplay. Students also create their own game concepts and GDDs and develop prototypes based on those. Prior video game experience is recommended but not required.

Course Learning Outcomes

- An understanding of the cognitive requirements, effective patterns, balance issues, and audience expectations that make a game "fun."

- Proficiency at evaluating and critiquing game titles and genres.

- The ability to create a game proposal for instructor review. Students will be exposed to professional game development engines and software.

Additional Learning Outcomes

- Create video games using a simple game development application.

- Deconstruct video games to create analog games that retain the essence of the original.

Materials

- There is no required textbook for this course.

- Internet articles and videos will be utilized as needed.

Schedule

Week 1—Introductions

- Tues: Introduce self and course; ask students their gaming background. Go over syllabus.
- Thurs: Game genres (class creates list) and Evolution of RPG Prezi (evolution of video games; Prezi too).
  - Quest 1: Critique the syllabus.

Week 2—Gamers

- Tues: Bartle's taxonomy, Quantic Foundry; introduce After-Action Report quest.
- Thurs: Game Design = crafting the player experience, Journalist's Questions, Honey Badger. What do players want (by genre)?
  - Quest 2: Analyze Self as Gamer.
    - Peer Reviews (2).
  - Quest 3: After-Action Report (due at the end of Week 4).
    - Peer Reviews (2).

Week 3—Games

- Tues: Discuss self-analyses. Game Systems and Game Mechanics.
- Thurs: Analyze *10,000,000 and Epistory* in class, using YouTube/LetsPlay videos.
  - Quest 4: Analyze a video game you're familiar with, discussing its systems and mechanics and how they work together to create the player experience.
    - Peer Reviews (2).

Week 4—Game Design

- Tues: My three definitions of game design. Elements of Game Design.
- Thurs: Discuss Flow in games. Discuss concept docs—capture the essence!

- Quest 3 (from Week 2): After-Action Report.

  - Peer Reviews (2).

Week 5—Pre-Production

- Tues: Introduce Scratch and teams. Show doc of links to games previous classes found. Talk about concept docs.

  - Teams can choose to use another game dev app—Twine, RPGMaker, etc.

- Thurs: Teams workshop and decide upon a game concept.

  - Quest 5: Create a one-page concept doc (using template) for a game you plan to create in Scratch (or other app).

    - Peer Reviews (2).

Week 6—Game Design Documents (GDDs)

- Tues: Discuss team concept docs—issues, suitability, etc. GDDs—building from concepts, place in game development.

- Thurs: Teams work on GDD together.

  - Quest 6: Write your GDD using provided template.

    - Peer Reviews (2).

Week 7—GDD Workshops

- Tues: GDD Workshops, groups of 3.

- Thurs: GDD Workshops, groups of 3.

  - Quest 7: Digital Game Prototype.

Week 8—Digital Game Prototype

- Tues: Playtesting and Feedback on Prototype.

  - Post feedback on DBs—takes place of peer reviews.

- Thurs: Playtesting and Feedback on Prototype.

  - Post feedback on DBs—takes place of peer reviews.

  - Quest 8: Digital Game Alpha.

Week 9—Digital Game Beta

- Tues: Playtesting and Feedback on Alpha.

    - Post feedback on DBs—takes place of peer reviews.

- Thurs: Playtesting and Feedback on Alpha.

    - Post feedback on DBs—takes place of peer reviews.

    - Quest 9: Digital Game Beta.

Week 10—Digital Game Gold Master

- Tues: Playtesting and Feedback on Beta.

    - Post feedback on DBs—takes place of peer reviews.

- Thurs: Playtesting and Feedback on Beta.

    - Post feedback on DBs—takes place of peer reviews.

    - Quest 10: Digital Game Gold Master.

Week 11—Devolver Project: Planning

- Tues: Devolver Project! Devolver team assignments. Devolver teams gather to discuss proposal and game design issues.

- Thurs: Devolver Project work.

    - Quest 11: Submit detailed Devolver Project proposal.

    - Peer Reviews (2).

Week 12—Devolver Project: Development

- Tues: Devolver Project work.

- Thurs: Devolver Project work.

    - No Quest due this week!

Week 13—Devolver Project: Alpha

- Tues: Devolver Project work.

- Thurs: Playtesting and Feedback on Devolver Project.

- Quest 12: Bring the initial version of Devolver game to class.

  - Written Game Feedback (into DB).

Week 14—Devolver Project: Beta

- Tues: Playtesting and Feedback on Devolver Project.
- Thurs: Playtesting and Feedback on Devolver Project.

  - Quest 13: Devolver Project Beta.

    - Written Game Feedback (into DB)

Week 15—Final Project and Final Class/Wrap-Up

- Tues: Final Playtesting and Feedback on Devolver Project.
- Thurs: Final class! Course wrap-up and feedback. Fill out evaluations.

  - Quest 14: Devolver Project Release Candidate.

    - Written Game Feedback (into DB).

  - Quest 15: Devolver Project Gold Master.

    - No DB feedback required!

  - Quest 16: Reflection Paper.

Grade Components (1,000 Points Total)

Attendance and Participation (peer reviews and DBs): 200 points.
  Quests 1–2, 4–9, 11–14, and 16: 40 points each (520 points total).
  Quest 3: 80 points.
  Quests 10 and 15: 100 points each (200 points total).
  TOTAL—1,000 points.

Attendance Policy

Attendance is part of your Participation grade. Miss more than one class and it will lower that grade. How much it lowers it depends on the other aspects of your participation—peer reviews, DB participation, playtesting and feedback, and so on.

SENIOR OVERVIEW SYLLABUS

Overview

Students use knowledge gained from previous courses in the curriculum to create a project of their own design. This capstone project showcases the student's skills and is aimed at helping the student gain the first step onto their desired career path. The student is responsible for creating a Milestone Map that lays out the tasks required to complete the project, as well as a planned schedule for when those tasks will be completed. The capstone project should become a centerpiece for the student's portfolio and may ultimately lead to a publishable game or game-related project.

Course Learning Outcomes

- Students are expected to tie together all their prior coursework from the Game Design program and apply it toward the creation of an individually designed, planned, and developed game project or senior thesis/research paper project.

- Students select a game project concept or research paper/thesis topic of their own design and develop it (including creation of and adherence to a project milestone map).

- Students demonstrate an understanding of the process of game design and documentation during the project's development or the creation of a well-researched and -written literature review and research proposal document.

Materials

- No textbook.

- Internet videos and articles as needed.

Schedule
Week 1—Starting Up

- Mon: Introduce course, self, go over syllabus—Prezi!

- Weds: Student (informal) presentation of senior project. Milestone Map discussion.

- Fri: Milestone Map discussion—problems, issues, etc.

  - Quest 1: Initial Milestone Map.

Week 2—Milestone Map Workshops

- Mon:—no class.
- Weds: Workshop—Milestone Map review and feedback.
- Fri: Workshop—Milestone Map review and feedback.
  - Quest 2: Milestone Map revision.

Week 3—Milestone Map Workshops

- Mon: Workshop—Milestone Map review and feedback.
- Weds: Workshop—Milestone Map review and feedback.
- Fri: Workshop—Milestone Map review and feedback.
  - Quest 3:
    - Group A, Presentation 1.
    - Group B, Presentation 1.

Week 4—Presentations, Round 1

- Mon: Group A Presentations.
- Weds: Group B Presentations.
- Fri: Overflow/Optional day—workshops, discussions.
  - Quest 4:
    - Group A, Presentation 2.
    - Group B, Presentation 2.

Week 5—Presentations, Round 2

- Mon: Group A Presentations.
- Weds: Group B Presentations.
- Fri: Overflow/Optional day—workshops, discussions.
  - Quest 5:
    - Group A, Presentation 3.
    - Group B, Presentation 3.

Week 6—Presentations, Round 3

- Mon: Group A Presentations.

- Weds: Group B Presentations.

- Fri: Overflow/Optional day—workshops, discussions.

  - Quest 6:

    - Group A, Presentation 4.

    - Group B, Presentation 4.

Week 7—Presentations, Round 4

- Mon: Group A Presentations.

- Weds: Group B Presentations.

- Fri: Overflow/Optional day—workshops, discussions.

  - Quest 7:

    - Group A, Presentation 5.

    - Group B, Presentation 5.

Week 8—Presentations, Round 5

- Mon: Group A Presentations.

- Weds: Group B Presentations.

- Fri: Overflow/Optional day—workshops, discussions.

  - Quest 8:

    - Group A, Presentation 6.

    - Group B, Presentation 6.

- Quest 9: Milestone Map Update (from all students).

Week 9—Presentations, Round 6

- Mon: Group A Presentations.

- Weds: Group B Presentations.

- Fri: Overflow/Optional day—workshops, discussions.
  - Quest 10:
    - Group A, Presentation 7.
    - Group B, Presentation 7.

Week 10—Presentations, Round 7

- Mon: Group A Presentations.
- Weds: Group B Presentations.
- Fri: Overflow/Optional day—workshops, discussions.
  - Quest 11:
    - Group A, Presentation 8.
    - Group B, Presentation 8.

Week 11—Presentations, Round 8

- Mon: Group A Presentations.
- Weds: Group B Presentations.
- Fri: Overflow/Optional day—workshops, discussions.
  - Quest 12:
    - Group A, Presentation 9.
    - Group B, Presentation 9.

Week 12—Presentations, Round 9

- Mon: Group A Presentations.
- Weds: Group B Presentations.
- Fri: Overflow/Optional day—workshops, discussions.
  - Quest 13:
    - Group A, Presentation 10.
    - Group B, Presentation 10.

Week 13—Presentations, Round 10

- Mon: Group A Presentations.

- Weds: Group B Presentations.

- Fri: Overflow/Optional day—workshops, discussions.

  - Quest 14:

    - Group A, Presentation 11. Due 4/22 by class time.

    - Group B, Presentation 11. Due 4/24 by class time.

Week 14—Presentations, Round 11

- Mon: Group A Presentations.

- Weds: Group B Presentations.

- Fri: Presentations.

  - Quest 15:

    - Group A, Presentation 12.

    - Group B, Presentation 12.

Week 15—Final Presentations, Round 12

- Mon: Group A Presentations.

- Weds: Group B Presentations.

- Fri: Group C Presentations.

- NOTE: These are formal presentations—a brief overview of your project, how it should help you land a job in your intended profession, and then show us what you've done over the past 15 weeks.

  - This presentation will be allotted 12–15 minutes. If there is not enough time to get all of them in, the last few presentations will be done next week.

  - Quest 16, Part 1: Final presentations.

Week 16—Course Wrap-Up, Feedback, Evaluations

- Mon: This class occurs during our scheduled final exam time. All students are expected to attend. This time will be used for presentations that did not fit in the previous week and for a post-mortem/wrapup of the class, with students giving feedback on what worked well for them and what could be improved.

  - Quest 16, Part 2: The final version of your project.

  - Quest 17: Reflection paper.

Grade Components (1,000 Points Total)

Attendance and Participation (including peer reviews): 240 points.
  Quests 1–15, 17: 40 points each (640 points total).
  Quest 16: 120 points.
  TOTAL—1,000 points possible.

Attendance Policy

Attendance is part of your Participation grade. Miss more than one class and it will lower that grade. How much it lowers it depends on the other aspects of your participation—peer reviews, DB participation, playtesting and feedback, and so on.

Appendix C

*Course Assignments
(Instructions and Templates)*

This section contains the assignment instructions and templates I created for my game design and narrative design classes. These can be used by instructors and students to guide the classroom learning experience and by individuals who want to build or enhance their game design or narrative design portfolios. The assignments here represent tasks I've performed many times as a game designer and narrative designer. These represent the type of work game studios look for from prospective employers.

Some assignments consist only of instructions to students, while others contain a template to help guide students in completing the assignment.

I hope these templates and assignment descriptions help others create or revise courses that they teach in narrative design and game design. I am also happy to receive feedback and suggestions at michaelbreault50@webster.edu.

NARRATIVE DESIGN I ASSIGNMENTS

This is the first in a two-course sequence on writing for games. The assignments (quests) are presented in the order in which students encounter them as the course progresses. One quest not listed here is Participation. This is a semester-long assignment that keeps track of students' attendance and participation in class discussions and activities.

All student work is reviewed in small-group workshops of three to four students after each assignment's due date, as outlined in Appendix B.

Student receive feedback from their peers on their writing and game design ideas. The last two assignments in this class involve revising previous work; earlier feedback from the instructor and peers helps students revise their work.

Concepts

In this class, students create three game design concepts, presenting each in a one-page concept document. A well-written concept document shows creativity and the ability to convert an idea into an outline for a game. These are abilities most game companies treasure in their employees. Feel free to use these templates as guides for developing concepts of your own.

Each of the three concepts outlines a very different type of game, as described below. Students use one of these concepts as the foundation for their work for the rest of the semester.

Quest 1—Concept Document #1 (Entertainment)

Create a one-page concept document for a game that you would be interested in working on. Use the Concept Document template below to guide your efforts. The italicized text in the template exists to help you fill out each section; be sure to delete it as you enter your content! Brevity is important here, so please *stick to one page.*

Note: Keep this concept doc to one (1) page. Be concise and decide what is most important to get across to your target audience (busy executives, bored marketing folks, and overworked game developers).

CONCEPT DOCUMENT TEMPLATE—ENTERTAINMENT GAME

GAME TITLE

Give your game a name! Leave this until after you've filled out the rest of the template.

INTENDED AUDIENCE

Who is your game intended for? Who will enjoy it?

HIGH CONCEPT

Describe your game in just a few sentences.

GENRE

What type of game is it? What sorts of games is it similar to?

DESCRIPTION

Describe the look and feel of your game. Briefly describe the game world, the player's place in it, and so on. Give more detail than in the "High Concept" section.

STORY

What is your game's story? Why is the player here and what are they doing? What is their eventual goal? (Even if your game doesn't have an explicit story, with characters and dialogue, it should have background and goal(s) for the player.)

SETTINGS/ENVIRONMENTS

List and briefly detail the setting(s)/environment(s) in which your game takes place. What will the player see in your game? Where will s/he go?

FEATURES/GAMEPLAY

List the important features of your game and give examples of its gameplay. This section should complement the "Description" section, not duplicate it. A bullet list would work well. How does this gameplay fit your story and setting?

USPs

What are your game's Unique Selling Points? What's different about it?

Quest 2—Arcade Game Short Story

Each student is to choose a classic, storyless arcade game and write a short story for it (at least two pages). This story should give a unique view of the main character's background, the game world/setting, and the main character's goals and motivations.

By "classic arcade game," I mean games like *Space Invaders*, *Pong*, *Defender*, *Frogger*, *Dig-Dug*, and so on.

This assignment is meant as an initial fiction-writing exercise for students, starting from the bare-bones plot of an arcade game.

Quest 3—Concept Document #2 (Serious/Educational)

Create another concept document, this time for an educational or serious game, using the template below. Be sure to discuss the learning content to be conveyed to the player.

Keep in mind that "educate" means to teach someone something useful to them. It's not necessarily a subject you'd take in school.

Note: Keep this concept doc to one (1) page. Be concise and decide what is most important to get across to your audience (busy executives, bored marketing folks, and overworked devs).

CONCEPT DOCUMENT TEMPLATE— EDUCATIONAL/SERIOUS GAME

GAME TITLE

Give your game a name! Leave this until after you've filled out the rest of the template.

INTENDED AUDIENCE

Who is your game intended for? Who will gain from the content you convey?

HIGH CONCEPT

Describe your game in just a few sentences. Include a mention of the content to be conveyed to the player.

GENRE

What type of game is it? What sorts of games is it similar to?

DESCRIPTION

Describe the look and feel of your game. Briefly describe the game world, the player's place in it, and so on. Give more detail than in the "High Concept" section.

STORY

Tell us about the story for your game. Why is the player here and what are they doing? What is their eventual goal? (Even if your game doesn't have an explicit story, with characters and dialogue, it should have background and goal(s) for the player.)

SETTINGS/ENVIRONMENTS

List and briefly detail the setting(s)/environment(s) in which your game takes place. What will the player see in your game? Where will s/he go?.

FEATURES/GAMEPLAY

List the important features of your game and give examples of its gameplay. This section should complement the "Description" section, not duplicate it. A bullet list might be the best way to present this information. How does this gameplay fit your content?

USPs

What are your game's Unique Selling Points? What's different about it?

Quest 4—Concept Document #3 (Game Adaptation)

Choose a novel, graphic novel, TV series, or movie that hasn't had a game adaptation created for it. Write up a concept doc treatment that adapts that property into a game format (entertainment, educational, or training). This document can be longer than one page but no more than two pages. Use this template to guide your treatment.

CONCEPT DOCUMENT TEMPLATE—GAME ADAPTATION

ORIGINAL IP (INTELLECTUAL PROPERTY)

Tell us about the property (movie, book, etc.) your game will be based on.

GAME WORLD/SETTING

Describe the world in which this property takes place.

INTENDED GAME GENRE

Tell us about the genre you have chosen for your game treatment of this property and why you feel it would be the best way to present this property in a game.

ORIGINAL STORY

Give us an overview of the original property's story. Then tell us if your game would enable the player to play through this story or experience parts of it, or if your game is intended to tell a completely different story. If the latter, explain how you plan to ensure your story stays true to the look and feel of the franchise, so that players don't feel misled.

YOUR STORY

Give us some of the major beats in your planned story so we get a feel for the player's experience. If it works best for you to merge this section with the previous one, feel free to do so.

ORIGINAL CHARACTERS

List the major characters in the original property, with brief descriptions of their personalities and roles in the story. Also mention what, if any, part these original characters will play in your story.

YOUR CHARACTERS

Tell us about the major characters in your story, giving us some detail about their backgrounds, personalities, and the roles they will fulfill in your game and story. Be sure to give us a good feel for your Hero and their nemesis (the Shadow).

AUDIENCE EXPECTATIONS

What do you feel the audience of the original property expects from a game adaption of it? How are you trying to meet (or distract the audience from) those expectations? What aspects of audience expectations do you feel would be most concerning or hardest to fulfill?

Quest 5—Game Design Document, Part 1

Choose one of your concept docs (from Quests 1, 3, or 4) from which to start developing an outline for a game design document (GDD). This quest is the first part of your GDD, covering your game's story, cast of characters, and game world; strive to make it as comprehensive as you can. Put your game's name in place of the current title of the GDD template.

The GDD is the foundation for subsequent development of your game's design and story, so make it good. Please note:

- Your cast of characters needs to include not just those on the side of the Hero, but also those on the Shadow's side as well.

- The Key Locations are places in your game world where important events occur. Don't just give the names of the places —give a brief description of the location and tell what happens there and why it's important to your story.

Use this template to guide your efforts (remember to delete italicized text as you go!)

GAME DESIGN DOCUMENT OUTLINE, PART 1 FOR

<<Name of Game>>

THE BASICS

(This information should mostly come from your concept doc.)

GAME

Describe your game in a paragraph.

GENRE

What genre does your game fit into?

AUDIENCE

Who is the target audience for your game?

UNIQUE SELLING POINT(S)

What is the hook(s) for your game? What's different about it? What's the player going to love about it? What is there about your game that will surprise the player and keep them coming back?

STORY

Here's where you give us the details on your game's story and the player's place in it. Every game needs a story, even if it's only for the dev team.

PLOT

What happens in your story? Give us at least a basic outline of your story, including the start and the ending.

THE PLAYER CHARACTER

Tell us who the player character (PC) is in your story—background, motivations, goals, and so on. If possible, include concept art of the PC or an image from another game to give us a sense of the PC.

THE FOE (SHADOW)

Who or what is the main force opposing the player's drive toward their end goal? What are this character's goals? How do they aim to achieve them?

OTHER CHARACTERS

Who else is in your story, what's their purpose, and what do they do?

STORY VEHICLES

Tell us how you will convey your story to the player. Will there be dialogue (text or voice) with non-player characters (NPCs)? Text screens with story as a reward for player accomplishments? Cutscenes?

THE GAME WORLD

Tell us about your game world here. Fill in all sections as completely as possible. Add other sections if your game calls for them.

ENVIRONMENTS

Describe the environments the player will encounter in your game. Concept art and/or images from other games could help convey this.

KEY LOCATIONS

Describe the key locations in your world, places where important parts of the story occur.

GAME FLOW

How does the PC experience your game world? How do the world's locations connect? Include the order in which the player encounters the sections of your game world. Note: Make sure the connections between areas are either logical or make sense within the context of your story!

INTERACTIVITY

What can the player do with your game world? How do they interact with it? List some examples of interactive objects, items, and locations here. Also, in what ways can the player interact with the inhabitants of your game world?

TRAINING

Is there a training level/area built into your game? If so, describe it here. If not, how does the player learn the controls and how to play? Does the training level also serve to familiarize the player with the game world and his/her PC?

MAP/LAYOUT

Describe the layout of your world here—how the levels, environments, or areas of your game world connect, how the player makes his/her way through your world. Include a map(s) or image(s) showing this layout.

Quest 6—Original Short Story

Write an original short story, 2–5 pages long, set in the game world you are developing. Remember that stories are about people/characters and how they cause or react to events in the world around them. Make this story about an important character or characters in your game. It can be about anyone in your world, not necessarily your game's Hero. This story should give the reader insight into your game world and the people who inhabit it.

Quest 7—Game Design Document, Part 2

This assignment is to complete Part 2 of the GDD started in Quest 5. Fill in the sections of the template below, completing the basic information needed for the design of your game. The GDD is the foundation for subsequent development of your game's design and story, so strive to make it as comprehensive as you can. Add Part 1 of your GDD to the front of Part 2, so your GDD is now complete, though in first-pass form.

GAME DESIGN DOCUMENT OUTLINE, PART 2

<<Name of Game>>

GAMEPLAY

This is the place to lay out your gameplay. How does the PC interact with your game world, its setting, characters, objects, structures, etc.? Tell us the major actions the player can take in your game. Add new categories below if your game design calls for them.

The reader should have a good sense of your intended player experience by reading this section.

PLAYER EXPERIENCE

What will the player experience be like in your game? What emotions or reactions are you aiming to inspire in the player?

PLAYER CHARACTER ACTIONS

What can the PC do in your game? How do they interact with the game world and its characters?

PLAYER CHARACTER END GOAL

What is the PC's end goal in the game? What are they trying to accomplish? And when they reach the end, what are the rewards?

ENEMIES

These are the animate obstacles to the player's progress. Who are the player's foes, what do they want, what do they do, etc.? Is there a hierarchy to these foes? If so, who leads them? Concept art or images from other games will help give a feel for these foes.

COMBAT

How does combat work? How does the player battle forces inimical to their quest? (It's OK if combat does not fit the theme of your game, but be sure to tell us what characters or objects oppose the player's quest and how they overcome them.)

OBSTACLES

What inanimate challenges will the player encounter in your game?

OBJECTS, ITEMS, WEAPONS, ETC.

What inanimate objects can the player pick up or otherwise interact with? How do those work? Any parts of the environment that are interactable, detail them here.

REPLAYABILITY

How replayable is your game? What makes it replayable? If it isn't, try to make it so.

ART STYLE/AESTHETICS

What is the look and feel of your game? What atmosphere do you hope to create for the player? Give some visuals of the environments in which your story and game will occur. Be sure to describe the images you add here, telling the environment artists and level designers on your team what each image means for the game.

Also be sure to give images for character art style.

Note: This section must include either original concept art or images/screenshots/concepts from other games that show the art style you're aiming for.

Create sub-sections here as needed.

USER INTERFACE/CONTROLS

How does the player interact with your game world and its characters, items, and environment? What information and capabilities do you provide the player as s/he is playing?

INTERFACE

What information will you display on-screen for the player? Include a sketch of the user interface (UI) during gameplay.

MENUS

What menus and capabilities do you provide the player (e.g., Inventory, Journal, Equipping/Loadout)? These should all be functions that enhance the player's experience. Include a sketch or image of each menu you plan.

MESSAGING

How does the game world convey information to the player? Is it via dialogue, text messages, verbal notifications, images and effects splashed onto the screen, etc.?

MUSIC AND SOUND EFFECTS

Tell us about the audio component of your game design. Keep in mind that audio works with the visuals, story, and gameplay to help create a unified theme for the player experience.

MUSIC

Describe the general style of the music for your game, the atmosphere you're trying to create, and the effect you hope the music has on the player. For each distinct area of your game, give suggestions as to the mood/atmosphere the music should convey.

SOUND EFFECTS

Give us an idea of the kinds of events, player/NPC actions, and so on that will trigger sound effects in your game. Also list unique ambient sounds (background sounds) for each distinct area of your game, to convey the feel of that area (e.g., machinery and truck sounds in an industrial area).

Quest 8—Story and Gameplay

In this assignment, take a step back from working on your GDD and consider how published games have integrated (or failed to integrate) story with gameplay. For a game of your choosing (default is *The Walking Dead*, Season 1 Episode 1), write a two- to four-page paper discussing how that development team integrated story and gameplay to create the player experience.

Think of this paper as a persuasive essay. State your thesis (whether or not this particular game did a good job of integrating story and gameplay) in the opening paragraph, present your evidence (give examples from the game to prove your point) in the middle sections of your paper, and then sum it all up for us with a concluding paragraph or two that restates your opinions about this game.

Note that the game you choose must have a significant story component!

Quest 9—Develop Story and Characters

Starting from the GDD Story sections in Quest 5 (story and characters), develop these sections much more fully. Give brief descriptions of the major beats or scenes of the story. You don't have to have the story completely fleshed out, just take it to the next stage of development, adding scenes and plot points.

Populate your story with a strong cast of characters, giving each a background, motivation(s), role(s) in the story, and relationships with other characters. Develop a strong cast on both sides of the story (the Hero's side and the Shadow's side). Make these characters come alive for us, make them feel like real people we'd care about instead of cardboard cutouts.

Put all this work in a separate "Story and Characters" doc. Put character information in a "Characters" section at the end of your doc.

There is no page limit to this assignment.

Quest 10—Cinematic Scripts

Write two cinematic scripts to accompany the game you're developing in your GDD. Use screenplay format. The first of these two scripts is for the opening cinematic of your game; the second script is for the ending cinematic of your game. Each should be 2–5 pages long.

As examples for my classes, I add links to the cinematic scripts I wrote for the *Punisher* game.

You can use brief scripts from the Internet as examples.

Keep in mind that your scripts should convey the information that artists, level designers, animators, sound designers, and other developers will need to create this cinematic.

Quest 11—Shadow Story

Next to the Hero, the Shadow is the most important character in your game's story. They may drive the story even more than the Hero.

For this assignment, write a two- to four-page story that gives new insight into the personality, motivation(s), and background of your Shadow. Let us see what makes them tick.

It doesn't matter whether you write your Shadow's story in first person or third person, as long as we get to see inside their mind. We need to see your Shadow as more than a cardboard cutout for the Hero's opposition to feel worthy of them.

Quest 12—Quest Documents

Develop three quests/missions for your game. Make sure that these complement your intended design and reveal both story and character to the player. These tasks should feel meaningful to the player (not just fetch quests), and they should advance the story. Ensure that the quests you create showcase the type of gameplay players can expect in your game.

Each quest should feature a different type of gameplay you intend for your game. One quest might center around exploration, another around solving a mystery by conversing with a series of NPCs, and a third by battling your way through foes.

Do not write out the actual dialogue to be said during the quest, just include a summary of the story and character information the player gains during the quest and who conveys it.

Use the following template to help guide your efforts. Feel free to make modifications if the format and content don't fit your intended quests.

QUEST TEMPLATE

Add a paragraph at the start of this doc that tells the reader the basics of your game—a few sentences on your game's genre, story, etc. to give the reader context for these quests.

QUEST NAME

Give your quest a name that hints at its purpose or end result, without being too obvious about it.

QUEST TYPE

What sort of quest is this—Kill, Fed Ex (delivery), etc.?

SUCCESS CRITERION/CRITERIA

What is the goal here, what does the player need to accomplish to succeed?

SETTING

Where does this quest take place, physically within your game world? How does this setting affect the player and quest?

PLACE IN STORY

Where in the overall course of the story does this quest occur?

CHARACTERS INVOLVED

List the characters the player will encounter during this quest, as well as the gameplay and/or story purpose each serves.

STORY PURPOSE

What part(s) of the story does the player experience during this quest? What is revealed to them or what do they learn?

GAMEPLAY PURPOSE

What obstacles/difficulties does this quest pose for the player? What skills, knowledge, or items do they need to use to fulfill this quest?

MISCELLANEOUS

Any information about your quest that doesn't fit the other categories, put it here.

QUEST PLAYTHROUGH

Walk us through this quest, from start to finish. Lay out each notable step in the quest, tell us where and when other characters are encountered, write out the conversations that occur, describe any obstacles the player encounters or discoveries they make, and so on. We should feel that we know everything about your quest by the end.

Here is a quest doc I created as an example for students

QUEST—AS I HANG DYING

QUEST NAME

As I Hang Dying

QUEST TYPE

This is an exploration quest undertaken to find certain artifacts. Combat and NPC interactions are central to the quest.

SUCCESS CRITERION/CRITERIA

The goal is to recover two priceless, magical artifacts—the sword and armor of the elven hero Vy'Lanarth.

SETTING

The quest begins at the Brown Viper Inn, in the town of Blackstone. The hero and companions journey to the Forest of Albareth. Deep within the forest lies the ruins of the ancient elven city of Za'Norum. Somewhere within these ruins lie the artifacts the hero seeks. The setting determines the journey the player must undertake to reach the goal, as well as the dangers encountered en route.

PLACE IN STORY

This quest is offered to the player midway through the game. It can be accepted any time the player is in the town of Blackstone and visits the Brown Viper Inn.

CHARACTERS INVOLVED

If the player chooses to attempt this quest, they are blessed (saddled?) with the following companions

Moosle—dwarven thief
Sir Regand—human paladin
Zirnal—human mage
Beattle—elven cleric
Vermile—orc druid
Damosur—halfling thief
Braston—human warrior

STORY PURPOSE

This quest leads the player to explore the lore and history of the Blackstone region. In the Forest of Albareth, the player encounters creatures unique to this area. Locals tell stories of the elves of the forest and their great city, now in ruins. Tales of the treasures lying within the ruins are told to entertain locals and visitors alike. If the player undertakes this quest, they discover the deadly dangers of the forest, and why the ancient elven treasures still remain there.

GAMEPLAY PURPOSE

This quest sends the player on a journey with several previously unknown companions. The player's interactions with them can determine how friendly they are, what information or backstory they divulge, and whether they run or fight when danger is encountered.

This quest highlights the mechanics of combat and exploration. Completing the quest grants the player two powerful magical artifacts and triggers an increase in the strength of combat foes.

QUEST PLAYTHROUGH

The player enters the village of Blackstone, hears of the Inn of the Brown Viper as a place to pick up local rumors.

At the inn, the PC overhears a local named Moosle talking of treasure awaiting those brave enough to explore the ancient elven city.

Several NPCs clamor to join Moosle in a quest to recover the treasures. The PC can join if they want.

If the PC joins, that completes the group listed above. The party sets off on its way.

A random encounter or two occur en route to the forest, a day's journey from Blackstone.

Once in the forest, the party follows a heavily overgrown path into the woods.

An hour later, a pack of giant spiders attacks the party.

Another hour of travel brings an encounter with a herd of centaurs, who immediately attack.

The party encounters a deep chasm, crossed only by a rickety wood-and-rope bridge.

While the party NPCs argue about whether to risk the crossing, a flock of harpies attacks, attempting to knock party members into the chasm.

If the party makes it across the bridge, the path leads them past a still-smoldering campfire. Getting within three feet of it releases a fire elemental that attacks the party.

Another hour along the path, the party enters the outskirts of the ruins of Za-Norum.

Exploring the ruins leads the party to the center of the ancient city. Random encounters enliven the exploration.

Finally the city's ancient treasury is found, deep underneath a building in the central square.

The treasure's guardian, a shadow elemental, must be defeated, tricked, or evaded to gain the fabled artifacts of Vy'Lanarth.

The route back to Blackstone is fraught with dangers equivalent to those encountered on the way in.

Quest 13A—Third Short Story

Write another original short story, 2+ pages long, that takes place in your game world. Remember that stories are about people/characters. Make this story about a character who is important to your story, but NOT your story's Hero or Shadow. Ideally the story will take place in an area of your game you have not yet explored in a previous story.

This story should give the reader more insight into your game world and the people who inhabit it.

Quest 13B—Revise Short Story

They say that writing is rewriting. Who says that? Everyone who writes for a living and cares about the quality of their work.

Pick one of the short stories you wrote earlier in this class and do a major revision of it. Use the feedback you received from me and from your classmates in workshops to help drive this revision. Your story should shine after this update!

Quest 14—Revise GDD

Now it's time to put it all together, to assemble all the pieces you've created for your game design. Use feedback you've received and new insights you've gained into your game to help you add more depth and detail to all the elements of your GDD. Every section of your GDD should be updated and expanded. Think of yourself as working to give the members of a dev team the information they need to begin developing your game.

I'm looking for a significant revision to all parts of your GDD here. Every section should be enhanced and expanded from its original state.

There is no page limit for this.

Quest 15—Reflection Paper

This is your final assignment. Write a two- to four-page paper reflecting on your experiences in this class—what you learned, what you liked the most about the course, what you liked the least, what you wished we had done, and any suggestions for improving the course. Tell me how things went for you in this course and how it compared to your expectations.

As with all feedback that you give, be sure to mention what you feel went well and what you think was helpful to you, as well as aspects of the course you feel could have been better. Any suggestions for improvement are welcome!

This shouldn't be an onerous chore, just tell me what went well and what didn't, what I should keep for future classes and what I should change.

NARRATIVE DESIGN II ASSIGNMENTS

This is the second in our two-course narrative sequence. This course focuses on students creating an Interactive Fiction (IF) game, usually in Twine2. The first four weeks are a collaborative experience in which students work in groups of four.

Quest 1—Interactive Fiction Concept Doc

Create a one-page concept document for an IF game that you want to work on. Use the Concept Document Template (given in Quest 1 of Narrative

Design I above) to describe your game concept. The italicized text in the template is there to help you fill out each section; delete it as you enter your content! Brevity is important, so stick to one page.

Note about the collaborative project: Each group of four students will finish the four-week beginning of class with four shared-world projects on which they have all collaborated.

In Week 1, everyone in the group creates a one-page concept document for an IF game. They review these for each other in a workshop, then each person's concept gets passed along to another member of the group who writes the story of that game (Quest 2). Those game stories are reviewed the following week and then each concept/story combination gets passed to the next person for the following week's assignment—to design a fitting game world for that concept and story (Quest 3). Those world docs are reviewed by the group and then each concept/story/world combination is passed along to the last person in each group who hasn't written anything for that particular combo. This person writes opening and ending cinematic scripts to begin and end the game's story (Quest 4).

At the end of the four-week collaborative project, each group has four sets of foundations for four IF games (concept, story, world, and scripts). And each person in the group has contributed a different piece to each game. Everyone wrote one concept doc, one story, one game world, and one set of cinematic scripts, but each of those tasks was for a different game.

The person who wrote each concept gets the four-doc set that started with that concept. This can be the start to their game's design, borrowing ideas from the contributions of their groupmates as they wish. This process emphasizes the collaborative nature of game development and the need to build on what others have done, rather than discard it and use only your own ideas.

Here are the next three assignments in this process.

Quest 2—Add a Story

Each student takes the concept doc from another student in their group and develops the game's story and a cast of characters to go with it. The resulting document (not including the original concept) should be two to six pages long.

Build upon what your classmate did in their concept doc. Remember that you are creating the story of the game, based on the brief plot blurb in the original concept. How does the story start, how does it end, and what happens in between those two points? Feel free to do this in bullet-point format if that's easier. This is a collaboration, so look to expand upon the work your classmate has done, *not* burn it down and start from scratch!

Also come up with a brief cast of characters for the game's story—Hero, Shadow, and the characters who support these two main characters.

Quest 3—Add a Game World

This week, each student takes the concept/story combo that others have worked on and add information about the setting for the game. Tell us about the game world in general, the regions the player encounters within it, and key locations in which important story or gameplay elements occur. It's your job to bring this game world to life!

Remember that the setting you create needs to fit with the game concept and story others have come up with. And ensure that it is appropriate for an IF game.

Quest 4—Add Cinematics

This is the final week of our collaborative project. This week, write the opening and ending cinematics for the game your groupmates have put together. Each student takes the concept/story/setting combo the others have worked on and writes two cinematic scripts. The first opens the game for the player, introducing them to the game world, PC, and starting situation. The second ends the game for the player, wrapping up the story and gameplay in a satisfying and rewarding way.

Once again, your work must build on the creative efforts of your groupmates. Make sure your work dovetails with theirs, leading the player into the story and game, and wrapping it up for them in a satisfying way.

Note that your IF game very likely won't have actual cinematics. But by creating these scripts, you're adding your thoughts on how you feel the game should be introduced to players and how it should end.

Quest 5—Analyze an Interactive Fiction Game

Play an IF game from the following list and write a two- to four-page analysis of its story and gameplay. Think about takeaways for the game you will create.

- Space Suit (http://ifdb.tads.org/viewgame?id=1mfe25emkc3o1eo9)

- Beneath Floes (https://bravemule.itch.io/beneathfloes)

- Adventure (http://ifdb.tads.org/viewgame?id=fft6pu91j85y4acv—click "Play Online")

- Roadwarden (https://moralanxietystudio.com/—scroll down to download the demo for your machine; not especially well-written but graphics make it a little more interesting)

- An IF game of your choice (must have story and player choice)

- Note that the Interactive Fiction Database (IFDB) site has lots of IF/ text adventure (TA) games to choose from!

Quest 6—Game Design Document (GDD)

Develop a GDD for an IF game. Start from either the concept you created for Quest 1 or a new concept you write up. Feel free to incorporate the ideas your groupmates added earlier for story, game world, and cinematics. Use the following template to guide your design planning.

IF GAME DESIGN DOCUMENT OUTLINE FOR

<<Name of Game>>

THE BASICS

GAME

Describe your game in a paragraph.

GENRE

What genre does your game fit into?

AUDIENCE

Who is the target audience for your game?

UNIQUE SELLING POINT(S)

What is the hook(s) for your game? What's different about it? What's the player going to love about it? What is there about your game that will surprise the player and keep them coming back?

STORY

Here's where you give us the details on your game's story and the player's place in it. Every game needs a story, even if it's only for the dev team.

PLOT

What happens in your story? Give us an outline of your story, including the start and the ending.

THE PLAYER CHARACTER

Tell us who the PC is in your story—background, motivations, goals, and so on. What is the PC trying to accomplish in your game?

THE FOE (SHADOW)

Who or what is the main force opposing the player's drive toward their end goal? What are this character's goals? How do they aim to achieve them?

OTHER CHARACTERS

Who else is in your story, what's their purpose, and what do they do?

GAMEPLAY

This is the place to lay out your gameplay. How does the PC interact with your game world and its characters? Tell us the major actions the player can take in your game. The reader should have a good sense of your intended player experience by reading this section.

PLAYER EXPERIENCE

What will the player experience be like in your game? What emotions or reactions are you aiming to inspire in the player?

PLAYER CHARACTER ACTIONS

What can the PC do in your game? How do they interact with the game world and its characters? What game mechanics are you hoping to incorporate into your IF game?

PLAYER CHARACTER END GOAL

What is the PC's end goal in the game? What are they trying to accomplish? And when they reach the end, what are the rewards?

ENEMIES

These are the animate obstacles to the player's progress. Who are the player's foes, what do they want, what do they do, etc.? Is there a hierarchy to these foes? If so, who leads them?

COMBAT

Will there be combat in your game? If so, how does it work? How does the player battle forces inimical to their quest? (It's OK if combat does not fit the theme of your game, but be sure to tell us what characters or objects oppose the player's quest and how they overcome them.)

OBSTACLES

What inanimate challenges will the player encounter in your game?

REPLAYABILITY

How replayable is your game? What makes it replayable? If it isn't, try to make it so.

THE GAME WORLD

Tell us about your game world here. Add other sections if your game calls for them. Remember that your descriptions of locations in your game will be the means you convey the look and feel of your game world to the player!

ENVIRONMENTS

Describe the environments the player will encounter in your game.

INTERACTIVITY

What can the player do with your game world? How do they interact with it? List some examples of interactive objects, items, and locations here.

KEY LOCATIONS

Describe the key locations in your world, places where vital parts of the story occur.

GAME FLOW

How does the PC experience your game world? How do the world's locations connect? Include the order in which the player encounters the sections of your game world. Note: Make sure the connections between areas are either logical or make sense within the context of your story!

MAP/LAYOUT

Include a map(s) or image(s) that visually depicts the layout of your game world as the player will experience it.

Quest 7—Flowchart

Flowchart a plan for how your game will be presented to players, detailing the player's path through the game's story, from room to room in your IF game. You can use Twine2 to quickly generate rooms to represent the pathways through your game or you can use a mapper app such as Trizbort (https://trizbort.genstein.net/). You are also free to draw your flowchart by hand, take a picture of it, and insert that picture into the document you submit.

Quest 8—Begin Development

Begin creating your IF game in Twine2. Use the plans you developed in your GDD but do not feel constrained by them. Your game will evolve well beyond those plans; that's part of the process of game development.

Quests 9–13—The Iteration Cycle: Playtesting and Revision

For the next several weeks, continue to develop your game. Each class period, all student games will be playtested by the class. Each week, your game is expected to be bigger and better than the previous week's version. Revision of text and ensuring sufficient player choice are critical to this effort.

Quest 14—Final IF Game

Turn in the final version of your IF game for this class.

Quest 15—Reflection Paper

See the Reflection Paper assignment (Quest 15) in the Narrative Design I class above.

ANALOG GAME DESIGN ASSIGNMENTS

In this class, students learn the principles of game design and then lay the plans to make an analog game (board game, card game, or tabletop role-playing game (RPG)) of their own. The latter half of the course is spent implementing those plans and bringing their games in for weekly playtesting. Every week, their games are expected to become more complete and polished.

Quest 1—Critique the Syllabus

Your first assignment is to wade into the dangerous wilderness of the course syllabus. Read it carefully. Try to find any mistakes, but also get a good feel for what we'll be doing this semester. Peruse the syllabus with the following guidelines in mind:

- Which week(s) do you think will be the most interesting?
- Which week(s) do you think will be the least interesting?
- What do you think will be your favorite assignment?
- What do you think will be your least favorite?
- Anything unexpected in the syllabus?
- Anything not there that you'd like to see?

Quest 2—Game Systems and Game Mechanics Analysis

Pick an analog game you played this week. Describe the game systems and game mechanics that combine to create the player experience, discuss how they interact, and suggest improvements to existing systems as well as new systems that could be added to improve the game.

Add in an "Advanced" or "Optional" layer of game mechanics that you feel would enhance the game for experienced players but still keep to the feel of the original mechanics.

Quest 3—Analyze Yourself as a Gamer

Write a two- to four-page paper analyzing yourself as a game player, using both Bartle's Taxonomy and the Quantic Foundry (QF) model (https://quanticfoundry.com/) to identify your motivations in a variety of game genres.

While analyzing yourself via Bartle's Taxonomy, consider your motivations in at least two or three different genres of games, either digital or analog. You should find that you have a different mix of motivations for each genre. *Be sure to give percentages for each motivation and make sure they add up to 100%!*

For the QF section of this quest: Go to the QF site. In the upper right corner, there's a link titled "Lab"; click on that link. Scroll down to the link to take the survey for the Board Games Motivation Profile (on the right side of the page). Click on that link and answer the survey questions.

At the end, you'll be shown a single chart with both primary and secondary motivations depicted on it. Read the explanations of the various motivations and what the chart tells you. Right click on the chart and save it or cut and paste it into the doc you're writing for Quest 3.

In your paper, end with a conclusion that tells us your thoughts on these two methods of analyzing yourself as a player. And tell us which method you think best represents your true player nature.

Quest 4—Concept Documents

Create two one-page concept documents for games that you would be interested in working on. This means *two completely separate* game ideas, each described in its own concept doc.

Use the Concept Document Template below to outline your game concept. The italicized text in the template exists to help you fill out each section; be sure to delete it as you enter your content! Brevity is important here, so stick to one page for each concept.

Remember: Keep each concept doc to one (1) page. And no cheating with tiny fonts or narrow margins! Be concise and decide what is most important to get across to your audience (busy executives, bored marketing folks, and overworked devs).

CONCEPT DOCUMENT TEMPLATE—ANALOG GAMES

GAME TITLE

Give your game a name! Leave this until after you've filled out the rest of the template.

INTENDED AUDIENCE

Who is your game intended for? Who will enjoy it?

HIGH CONCEPT

Describe your game in just a few sentences.

GENRE

What type of game is it? What sorts of games is it similar to?

DESCRIPTION

Describe the look and feel of your game. Briefly describe the game world, the player's place in it, and so on. Give more detail than in the "High Concept" section.

STORY

What is your game's story? Why is the player here and what are they doing? What is their eventual goal? (Even if your game doesn't have an explicit story, with characters and dialogue, it should have background and goal(s) for the player.)

SETTINGS/ENVIRONMENTS

List and briefly detail the setting(s)/environment(s) in which your game takes place. What will the player see in your game? Where will they go?

FEATURES/GAMEPLAY

List the important features of your game and give examples of its gameplay. This section should complement the "Description" section, not duplicate it. A bullet list would work well. How does this gameplay fit your story and setting?

USPS

What are your game's Unique Selling Points? What's different about it?

FORMAT

Is the game you'll develop in this class a board game, card game, hybrid, RPG, or of another type?

Quest 5—GDD, Initial Pass

Starting from one of the concept docs you wrote, create a GDD for that game, using the template provided below. While this is your first pass at detailing out your intended game, make it as comprehensive as possible. You will revise and expand this in the next assignment based on feedback from your classmates and instructor.

GAME DESIGN DOCUMENT OUTLINE FOR

<<Name of Game>>

THE BASICS

(Most of this page should come from your concept doc.)

GAME

Describe your game in a paragraph.

TYPE & GENRE

What type of game is it (board game, card game, RPG, hybrid, etc.)? What genre does your game fit into?

AUDIENCE

Who is the target audience for your game?

UNIQUE SELLING POINT(S)

What is the hook(s) for your game? What's different about it? What's the player going to love about it? What is there about your game that will surprise the player and keep them coming back?

STORY

Here's where you tell us what you game's about and what players' goals are in the game. Every game needs a story, even chess has a story.

BACKSTORY

What has transpired to bring the game to the point at which players enter the game? What's the story or your game and how do the players come into that story?

PLAYERS AND THEIR GOALS

What are players trying to do in your game? What role(s) do they take on and what is their ultimate goal? (For example, in Monopoly players take on the roles of would-be landlords, trying to buy up all the property they can. Their eventual goal is to drive all the other players into bankruptcy.)

OTHER STORY ELEMENTS

If your game has other story elements, describe them here.

GAMEPLAY

This is the place to lay out your gameplay. What can players do in your game? How do they interact with each other? What things can happen to players in your game? The reader should have a good sense of your intended player experience by reading this section.

GAMEPLAY BASICS

Give us an overview of the primary gameplay in your game. (For example, in Risk, the primary gameplay is battling with other players for control of territory on the game board.)

GAME SYSTEMS

Tell us about the game systems in your game, with a very brief description of each. (For example, Movement is a system in most games. Combat or Conflicts among Players is another.)

GAME MECHANICS

For each game system mentioned above, tell us how it works. (For example, the movement system in Monopoly works by players rolling two dice and moving that number of spaces around the board and then interacting with the space they end up with in a variety of ways.)

PLAYER INTERACTIONS

Analog games gather people around a table to play. Thus the interactions among players are critical to analog gameplay. Briefly describe all the ways in which players interact in your game.

CHALLENGES

What challenges are there for players in your game?

ITEMS AND EQUIPMENT

What inanimate objects can the player pick up or otherwise interact with? How do those work? Any parts of the game's environment that are interactable, detail them here.

GAMEPLAY EXAMPLE

Tell us what happens on a player's turn, what actions they can do, how a player's turn might proceed.

REPLAYABILITY

How replayable is your game? What makes it replayable?

PHYSICAL COMPONENTS

Tell us as much as you can about the physical components (game board, cards, pieces, etc.) that you plan for your game. Add other sections if your game calls for them.

GAME BOARD

Will your game have a physical board, either one that's always the same or one that can vary from game to game? If it has a board, tell us about it.

CARDS

Tell us about any cards you are planning on having in your game. What is their purpose in the game, what do they do, and so on.

OTHER COMPONENTS

What else might there be to the physical components of your game? Are there character pieces, armies, tokens, currency, and so on?

GAME BOARD LAYOUT

If your game has a board, add a preliminary sketch of it here. You can roughly sketch it by hand, take a picture of it, and embed that picture here. Or you can sketch it in Paint or some other app.

ART STYLE/AESTHETICS

What is the look and feel of your game? Add some visuals that give us an idea of the art style you are thinking of for your game. This can be either original concept art or images/screenshots from other games that show the art style you're aiming for.

Quest 6—GDD, Second Pass

For this assignment, revise and expand upon the GDD you started in Quest 5. You've received feedback on your design plans; use that feedback to fill holes, add missing mechanics, and expand your game design. Every section of your original GDD should see further development. Get your GDD to the point where it can be used as the foundation upon which you build your game.

Quest 7—Initial Prototype

You've made your plans and have received feedback on them. Spend this week getting your game ready for others to playtest.

A week is a very short time to get all the mechanics of a game ready to playtest. Think about the mechanic(s) that is truly the core of your game-play and work on getting that playable first. In the coming weeks, add new functionality to your game each week while simultaneously revising and improving existing mechanics.

Note: Your game must have a set of written rules for players! Here is a list of guidelines for your rules.

GAME RULES

The following elements should be present in your game rules. Separate the sections of rules by using the section names as headers (e.g., Story/Intro, Component List, and so on).

SECTIONS

Story/Intro—what players are doing, what their goals are
Component List—all the parts of your game
Setup—how to set up and get ready to play
How to Start—how to begin play
Turn Sequence—what a player can do on their turn
How to Play—details about how the game mechanics work
How to Win—wrap up with the victory conditions, very specifically how to win your game
Advanced/Optional Rules—more game mechanics players can decide to layer in once they've mastered the Basic game.

GENERAL THOUGHTS

Start with a brief story for the players—what the game's about, what they're doing in the game, and what their goal(s) is.

> Be sure to state players' goals are in the game!
> Don't need to be flowery or fiction-y, just what the game's about.

Think about what players need to know to play your game

> What do they need to know first? That's where you start after the brief intro
> Setup

General rules about how to play
The order in which players do things in their turn

Keep your rules concise, direct, and to the point!

Don't being cute, put the rules in a character's voice, or anything like that.
Keep your sentences and paragraphs short!
Outline form (bullet points) is fine at this stage

As with everything else about your game at this point, you're going to get lots of feedback and make lots of changes.

Don't worry about making the rules perfect, just make them understandable

Decide what game mechanics are core to your gameplay

That becomes your Basic game

Everything else is layers you can add later, perhaps as Optional or Advanced rules that players can add in as they master the Basic rules.
At this point, work on getting the Basic rules into your rulesheet. The rest can come later, as you get feedback, fix problems, and iterate on your game.

Quests 8–14—The Iteration Cycle: Playtesting and Revision

For the next several weeks, continue to develop your game, using feedback to drive improvement. Each class period, all student games will be playtested by the class. Each week, your game is expected to be better and more complete than the previous week's version. Refinement of your game's rules is also expected.

Quest 15—Final Game and Revised GDD

This is it. The final, ultimate version of your game, complete with one printed copy of your game's rules. The second part of this assignment is an updated version of your GDD. You need to revise and update it to reflect the final state of your game. Incorporate any changes and enhancements you've made over the last eight weeks; there should be a lot of them. Ideally you have been working on revising your GDD for a couple of weeks now.

A revised GDD that presents the design of a well-tested game is a valuable addition to the portfolio site of anyone who would like to break into the game industry. Do a good job on this.

If there are aspects of your game that you were not able to get to, you can put those in notes at the end of your GDD, in a "Future Revisions" section.

Quest 16—Reflection Paper

See the final assignment in the Narrative Design I class above.

WORLD DESIGN ASSIGNMENTS

Quest 1—World Design Analysis

Choose a digital game to analyze, focusing on its world design—setting, story, characters, conflicts, action, and events that bring that world to life for players. Write a 2–5 page paper analyzing these aspects of that game's design.

Write your paper assuming the reader has never played this game. Don't go into excruciating detail but make sure we get the major points.

To help guide your analysis, use the questions here.

GAME WORLD ANALYSIS PROMPTS

Consider the following aspects of your chosen game as you write up your analysis. Remember that any point you make should be backed up with a concrete fact or example. The questions below are not for you to answer with robotic yes or no replies; they are to help guide you in describing this game's world and its impact on the player experience.

SETTING

What is the physical setting for this game?
What type of world is it, what terrains and biomes does the player encounter?
How do the terrain and physical layout of this game world affect its mood/atmosphere?
Tell us about some of the important locations in the game world.
How does the setting affect or interact with the story and characters?

In a well-developed game, the setting is a vital part of the story, often feeling like a character in the story, so strong is its presence. (Think of the Overlook Hotel in *The Shining* movie.) How well does the setting of your chosen game do this?

Story—What's the game's story? Give us the overall plot in a few paragraphs.

Characters—Tell us (briefly) about the main characters in the story, what parts they play in the story and gameplay, how well-developed they feel, and what interactions the player has with them. Who is the player in this game?

CONFLICT

What is the main conflict in the game?
Who drives this conflict, who are the major characters in it?
What is the player's part in this conflict? Does it feel like the player has any agency (free will) in the story or is s/he have little to no effect on it?
What smaller conflicts (sub-plots) are in the game?

Events—What major events occur in the story and how much of a part does the player play in them? What does each major event mean for the direction of the story and the player?

Conclusion—Wrap it all up for us in a concluding paragraph. How do all the elements you've discussed work together to deliver the player experience?

You don't have to slavishly follow the above prompts, nor tackle them in the given order. Feel free to write your analysis in whatever manner seems most appropriate to you.

Quest 2—Analyze Yourself as a Gamer

Write a 2–4 page paper analyzing yourself as a game player, using both Bartle's Taxonomy and the QF model (https://quanticfoundry.com/) to identify your motivations in a variety of game genres.

While analyzing yourself via Bartle's Taxonomy, consider your motivations in at least two or three different genres of games, either digital or analog. You should find that you have a different mix of motivations for each genre. *Be sure to give percentages for each motivation and make sure they add up to 100%!*

In your paper, end with a conclusion that tells us your thoughts on these two methods of analyzing yourself as a player. And tell us which method you think best represents your true player nature.

Quest 3—Concept Docs

Create two *one-page* concept documents for game worlds that you would be interested in working on. This means two completely separate ideas, each described in its own concept doc.

Use the Concept Document Template below for each concept. The italicized text in the template exists to help you fill out each section; be sure to delete it as you enter your content! Brevity is important here, so *stick to one page* for each concept.

Note: Keep each concept doc to one (1) page. And no cheating with tiny fonts or narrow margins! Be concise and decide what is most important to get across to your audience (busy executives, bored marketing folks, and overworked devs).

CONCEPT DOCUMENT TEMPLATE—GAME WORLD

WORLD TITLE

Give your world a name! You can leave this until after you've filled out the rest of the template, if need be.

INTENDED AUDIENCE

Who is your world intended for—what type of gamers? What will your game deliver that will engage this audience?

HIGH CONCEPT

Describe your game world in just a few sentences.

DESCRIPTION

Describe the look and feel (atmospheric details) of your game world. Briefly describe the setting, the player's place in it, and so on. Give more detail than in the "High Concept" section.

STORY

What is the story of your world? What's going on in the world that will affect the player's experience? Why is the player here and what are they doing? What is their eventual goal?

SETTINGS/ENVIRONMENTS

List and briefly detail at least some of the setting(s)/environment(s) in your world. What will the player see in your world? Where will they go?

FEATURES/GAMEPLAY

List the important gameplay features of your world. This section should complement the "Description" section, not duplicate it. A bullet list would work well. How does this gameplay fit your story and setting?

USPS

What are your game world's Unique Selling Points? What's different about it from worlds players might have experienced in other games?

Quest 4—GDD, Part 1

Choose one of the concept docs you created and developing the beginnings of an outline for a GDD. Use the template below to guide your efforts. This will be the first part of your GDD, covering your game world's story, cast of characters, and setting; strive to make it as comprehensive as you can. And put at least a tentative name for your world in place of the current title of the GDD template.

The GDD is the foundation for subsequent development of your world's design and story, so make it good. Give your classmates some solid info and ideas to react to.

Here is the template for Part 1 of your GDD:

GAME DESIGN DOCUMENT OUTLINE, PART 1 FOR

<<Name of Game World>>

THE BASICS

(This information should mostly come from your concept doc.)

YOUR WORLD

Describe your game world in a paragraph.

AUDIENCE

Who is the target audience for your game? What do they want in this sort of game?

Unique Selling Point(s)

What is the hook(s) for your game world? What's different about it? What's the player going to love about it? What is there about your world that will surprise the player and keep them coming back?

STORY

Here's where you give us the details on your world's story and the player's place in it. Every game project needs a story, even if it's only for the dev team.

Plot

What happens in your story? Give us at least a basic outline of your story, including the start and the ending.

The Player Character

Tell us who the PC is in your story—background, motivations, goals, and so on. If possible, include concept art of the PC or an image from another game to give us a sense of the PC.

The Foe (Shadow)

Who or what is the main force opposing the player's drive toward their end goal? What are this character's goals? How do they aim to achieve them?

Other Characters

Who else is in your story, what's their purpose, and what do they do?

Story Vehicles

Tell us how you will convey your story to the player. Will there be dialogue (text or voice) with NPCs? Text screens with story as a reward for player accomplishments? Cutscenes?

THE WORLD

Tell us about your world (setting) here. Fill in all sections as completely as possible. Add other sections if your game calls for them.

Environments

Describe the environments the player will encounter in your world. Concept art and/or images from other games could help convey this.

KEY LOCATIONS

Describe the key locations in your world, places where important parts of the story occur.

DENIZENS

Tell us about the inhabitants of your game world. What sorts of creatures, monsters, and people live there? And where do they live? If you wish, you can incorporate this information into the "Environments" section, listing the inhabitants of each area of your game world.

GAME FLOW

How does the PC experience your game world? How might your world's story unfold for the player? Note: Make sure the connections between areas are either logical or make sense within the context of your story!

INTERACTIVITY

What can the player do in your world? How do they interact with it? List some examples of interactive objects, items, and locations here. Also, in what ways can the player interact with the inhabitants of your world?

MAP/LAYOUT

Describe the layout of your world here—how the areas connect, how the player makes their way through your world. Include a map(s) or image(s) showing this layout. If you include a rough map here, it will help reviewers get a better sense of your game's setting. (A map isn't required for the first pass at this section of your GDD, but it will be looked for when you do your revision pass over your completed GDD.)

Quest 5—GDD, Part 2

This week's assignment is to complete Part 2 of your GDD. Fill in the sections of the template below, completing the basic information needed for the design of your game. The GDD is the foundation for subsequent development of your game's design and story, so strive to make it as comprehensive as you can.

For completeness' sake, take Part 1 of your GDD and add it to the front of Part 2. So your doc is now your complete GDD (Part 1 and Part 2) together. You are free to take an editing pass over Part 1 (story, characters, and game world), but your grade for this assignment will be strictly the work you do on Part 2. Email me if you have any questions about this.

Here is the template for Part 2 of your GDD.

GAME DESIGN DOCUMENT OUTLINE, PART 2 FOR

<<Name of Game>>

GAMEPLAY

This is the place to lay out your gameplay. How does the PC interact with your game world's setting, characters, objects, events, etc.? Tell us the major actions the player can take in your design. Add new categories below if your design calls for them. The reader should have a good sense of your intended player experience by reading this section.

PLAYER EXPERIENCE

What will the player experience be like? What emotions or reactions are you aiming to inspire in the player?

PLAYER CHARACTER ACTIONS

What can the PC do in your world? How do they interact with the game world and its characters?

PLAYER CHARACTER END GOAL

What is the PC's end goal? What are they trying to accomplish? And when they reach the end, what are the rewards?

ENEMIES

These are the animate obstacles to the player's progress. Who are the player's foes, what do they want, what do they do, etc.? Is there a hierarchy to these foes? If so, who leads them? Concept art or images from other games will help give a feel for these foes.

COMBAT

How does combat work? How does the player battle forces inimical to their quest? (It's OK if combat does not fit the theme of your world, but be sure to tell us what characters or objects oppose the player's quest and how they overcome them.)

OBSTACLES

What inanimate challenges will the player encounter in your world (e.g., puzzles, physical barriers to overcome, and so on)?

OBJECTS, ITEMS, WEAPONS, ETC.

What inanimate objects can the player pick up or otherwise interact with? How do those work? Any parts of the environment that are interactable, detail them here.

REPLAYABILITY

How replayable is your world? What makes it replayable? If it isn't, try to make it so.

ART STYLE/AESTHETICS

What is the look and feel of your game world? What atmosphere do you hope to create for the player? Give some visuals of the environments in which your story will occur. Be sure to describe the images you add here, telling the environment artists and level designers on your team what each image means.

Also be sure to give images for character art style.

Note: This section must include either original concept art or images/screenshots/concepts from other games that show the art style you're aiming for. Create sub-sections here as needed.

USER INTERFACE/CONTROLS

How does the player interact with your world and its characters, items, and environment? What information and capabilities do you provide the player as they are playing? Think about your UI and give us details about it here.

INTERFACE

What information will you display on-screen for the player? Include a sketch of the UI during gameplay. Note that different situations often require different interfaces. The UI for combat would differ greatly from that for conversation, which would in turn differ greatly from that for puzzle-solving. Think about what the player will be able to do in your game and what sort of interface would best convey the information they need.

MENUS

What menus and capabilities do you provide the player (e.g., Inventory, Journal, Equipping/Loadout)? These should all be functions that enhance the player's experience. Include a sketch or image of each menu you plan.

MESSAGING

How does the game world convey information to the player? Is it via dialogue, text messages, verbal notifications, images and effects splashed onto the screen, etc.?

MUSIC AND SOUND EFFECTS

Tell us about the audio component of your design. Keep in mind that audio works with the visuals, story, and gameplay to help create a unified theme for the player experience.

MUSIC

Describe the general style of the music for your game, the atmosphere you're trying to create, and the effect you hope the music has on the player. For each distinct area of your world, give suggestions as to the mood/atmosphere the music should convey.

SOUND EFFECTS

Give us an idea of the kinds of events, player/NPC actions, and so on that will trigger sound effects in your game world. Also list unique ambient sounds (background sounds) for each distinct area, to convey the feel of that area (e.g., machinery and truck sounds in an industrial area).

Quest 6—GDD Revision

You have now worked on both Parts 1 and 2 of your GDD. Ideally, you've already used feedback to get a start on revising your GDD.

Now take a good, hard pass over your entire GDD. Expand upon the ideas you wrote up earlier, fix the holes others have pointed out, and develop your game world design as fully as you can. This is the final pre-production stage of your game's development, so be as thorough as you can. Changes made at this stage are still cheap and easy. Changes made once you begin creating your game will be much harder and more time consuming.

If you have ideas you're not sure of, still get them into this GDD revision so others can give you feedback on them. Put questions in there for your reviewers to help you with.

Quest 7—Initial Game World Implementation

This quest represents the transition from pre-production to production. Now's the time to begin implementing the design plans you've laid out over the last few weeks.

Using the game development application you have chosen (such as RPGMaker, Unity, Unreal, and so on), create an initial pass at your intended game. At the very least, have a rough layout of the world for reviewers to explore and give you helpful feedback on.

You should be presenting a significant chunk of your game world here—it could be lots of roughed-in terrain and buildings, or a small section with NPCs with scripting and dialogue, or some other combination. It's not expected to be polished or anywhere near finished quality, just a good amount of work that you can get reviewers we can give you feedback on.

Quests 8–12—Playtesting and Revision

Each week, bring to class a noticeably better version of your game world— larger, with more content, and with increasing polish. Your game will be playtested by classmates every week. They will supply feedback that will help you improve your game world.

Quest 13—Final Version of Your Game World

In the last week of class, turn in the final version of the game world you've been building all these weeks. There will be one final round of playtesting, for students to give you a last set of feedback.

Quest 14—Updated GDD and Reflection Paper

Revise the GDD you created long ago to reflect the final state of your game. Incorporate any changes and enhancements you've made over the last eight weeks; there should be a lot of them.

A revised GDD that accurately represents the design foundation of the game you've been making over the last weeks is a valuable addition to the portfolio site of anyone who would like to break into the game industry. Accompanied by your concept doc (take an editing pass at this too) and your actual game, these three elements show your progress from initial idea to implementation. Do a good job on this.

If there are aspects of your game that you were not able to get to, you can put those in notes at the end of your GDD, in an "Upcoming Revisions" section.

For the Reflection paper part of this assignment, see the final assignment in the Narrative Design I class above.

INTRODUCTION TO DIGITAL GAME DESIGN ASSIGNMENTS

These assignments are for an introductory course that I teach in digital game design at Webster University. Students in this class have little to no experience making games but end up with pieces for their portfolios.

Quest 1—Analyze Yourself as a Gamer

Write a two- to four-page paper analyzing yourself as a game player, using both Bartle's Taxonomy and the QF model (https://quanticfoundry.com/) to identify your motivations in a variety of game genres.

While analyzing yourself via Bartle's Taxonomy, consider your motivations in at least two or three different genres of games, either digital or analog. You should find that you have a different mix of motivations for each genre. *Be sure to give percentages for each motivation and make sure they add up to 100%!*

In your paper, end with a conclusion that tells us your thoughts on these two methods of analyzing yourself as a player. And tell us which method you think best represents your true player nature.

Quest 2—After-Action Report

For this assignment, students play a digital game of their choice in its entirety, keeping a log of gameplay times, experiences, and thoughts. Upon finishing the game, they write a five- to six-page report that includes a summary of their play log.

This is given as a three-week-long assignment. Students are advised not to wait until the last couple of days to begin it, as this assignment should take 10 or more hours to complete (between playing the game, recording play sessions, and writing an analysis of your experience).

Use this template as a guide to writing the report.

AFTER ACTION REPORT (AAR) TEMPLATE

For the next three weeks, play a digital game of your choice. Pick a game that will take you at least 10–20 hours to play. Do not choose a game that is too simple or easy. Try to pick a game you haven't played before or haven't completed.

Try to finish your chosen game in the next three weeks so you can give a full report of it from start to finish.

Follow this organization when you make your report.

SECTION 1: OVERVIEW

Name of the game you played, year it was published, who made it.

Give a brief overview of the game—what sort of game it is, why you chose to play it, etc.

Who is the audience for this game, who is the game aimed at?

Roughly how many hours you spent playing the game.

SECTION 2: GAMEPLAY RECORD

In this section, keep a record of your gameplay times. Write down the day, time you started playing, and time you stopped. Then write some notes about what you did in the game each time you played.

For example

Sunday, February 21, 2018: Started at 11:15AM, Stopped at 2:00PM (2.75 hours played). Began in World 2–2. Killed about 60 foes, gained 11 coins. Died five times, got frustrated and threw the controller twice. Found three secret rooms. Completed World 2–2 after two hours, started in on World 2–3. Got about halfway through, had to quit for class.

Keep a record of every gameplay session and what happened. Tell us how you felt about what was happening on the screen and any thoughts you had about what happened, what could have gone better, anything you learned, and so on. If there are story elements to the game, tell us what parts of the story you experienced.

SECTION 3: CONCLUSION

In this section, sum up your gameplay experience. Did you enjoy this game? How did it end? What did you like about it? What didn't you like about it? Make suggestions for improving the parts of the game you didn't like.

This section should be 1–2 pages of your thoughts on the game, its story and gameplay. Don't just write a simple summary here—add your thoughts on what you experienced, how you felt about it, what you liked and didn't like, and so on.

Quest 3—Digital Game Analysis

Choose a digital game of sufficient complexity (i.e., at least five major game systems) and write a 2–3 page analysis of it. Games like *Plants vs. Zombies* or *10,000,000* would be fine; feel free to choose any reasonably complex game you wish.

Give a general overview of the game, then describe the game systems, how they operate, how they interact, and how each affects gameplay.

Make suggestions for improvements to existing systems or systems that might be added to improve the player experience.

Use the prompts here to guide your paper.

DIGITAL GAME ANALYSIS—PROMPTS

Consider the following aspects of your chosen game as you write up your analysis

The Basics—game name, developer, genre, game overview, etc.

The Purpose—What do players do in this game, what are their goals?

Story—What's the game's story? (All games have a story, even if it's just a recap of what the player is after in the game.)

Interactions—If this is a multiplayer game, what interactions occur among players? If it's a single-player game, what interactions does the PC have with NPCs?

Gameplay—Tell us about the mechanics of the game, how the game works. What systems or mechanics are core to the experience (e.g., in Mario Kart the core mechanics are driving around the track, picking up and using power-ups, and interacting with other players/AI)? Any ideas for game mechanics you'd like to see added to this game?

The Good, the Bad, and the Ugly—what do you like about the game and what do you dislike? What areas do you see for improvement, what do you wish the developers had incorporated into the game?

Sum Up Your Experience—How do you feel about the game and why? Wrap it all up for us in a concluding paragraph.

Note that you don't have to slavishly follow the above prompts, nor tackle them in the given order if you do follow them. Feel free to write your game analysis in whatever manner seems most appropriate to you.

Quest 4—Concept Document

Create a one-page concept document for a game that you would be interested in building in a digital development application of your choice.

Use the Concept Document Template below to describe your game concept. The italicized text in the template exists to help you fill out each section; be sure to delete it as you enter your content! Brevity is important here, so stick to one page.

Note: Be concise and decide what is most important to get across to your audience (busy executives, bored marketing folks, and overworked devs).

CONCEPT DOCUMENT TEMPLATE

GAME TITLE

Give your game a name! Leave this until after you've filled out the rest of the template.

INTENDED AUDIENCE

Who is your game intended for? Who will enjoy it?

HIGH CONCEPT

Describe your game in just a few sentences.

GENRE

What type of game is it? What sorts of games is it similar to?

DESCRIPTION

Describe the look and feel of your game. Briefly describe the game world, the player's place in it, and so on. Give more detail than in the "High Concept" section.

STORY

What is your game's story? Why is the player here and what is s/he doing? What is his/her eventual goal? (Even if your game doesn't have an explicit story, with characters and dialogue, it should have background and goal(s) for the player.)

SETTINGS/ENVIRONMENTS

List and briefly detail the setting(s)/environment(s) in which your game takes place. What will the player see in your game? Where will s/he go?

FEATURES/GAMEPLAY

List the important features of your game and give examples of its gameplay. This section should complement the "Description" section, not duplicate it. A bullet list would work well. How does this gameplay fit your story and setting?

USPs

What are your game's Unique Selling Points? What's different about it?

Quest 5—Game Design Doc

Starting from the concept doc you wrote, create a GDD for your game, using the template provided below. While this is your first pass at detailing out your intended game, make it as comprehensive as possible. This will be the foundation upon which you create your game.

GAME DESIGN DOCUMENT OUTLINE FOR

<<Name of Game>>

THE BASICS

GAME

Describe your game in a paragraph.

GENRE

What genre does your game fit into?

AUDIENCE

Who is the target audience for your game?

UNIQUE SELLING POINT(S)

What is the hook(s) for your game? What's different about it? What's the player going to love about it? What is there about your game that will surprise the player and keep them coming back?

STORY

Here's where you give us the details on your game's story and the player's place in it. Every game needs a story, even if it's only for the dev team.

PLOT

What happens in your story? Give us at least a basic outline of your story, including the start and the ending.

THE PLAYER CHARACTER

Tell us who the PC is in your story—background, motivations, goals, and so on. If possible, include concept art of the PC or an image from another game to give us a sense of the PC.

THE FOE (SHADOW)

Who or what is the main force opposing the player's drive toward their end goal? What are this character's goals? How do they aim to achieve them?

OTHER CHARACTERS

Who else is in your story, what's their purpose, and what do they do?

STORY VEHICLES

Tell us how you will convey your story to the player. Will there be dialogue (text or voice) with NPCs? Text screens with story as a reward for player accomplishments? Cutscenes?

GAMEPLAY

This is the place to lay out your gameplay. How does the PC interact with your game world, its setting, characters, objects, structures, etc.? Tell us the major actions the player can take in your game. Add new categories below if your game design calls for them.

The reader should have a good sense of your intended player experience by reading this section.

PLAYER EXPERIENCE

What will the player experience be like in your game? What emotions or reactions are you aiming to inspire in the player?

PLAYER CHARACTER ACTIONS

What can the PC do in your game? How do they interact with the game world and its characters?

PLAYER CHARACTER END GOAL

What is the PC's end goal in the game? What are they trying to accomplish? And when they reach the end, what are the rewards?

ENEMIES

These are the animate obstacles to the player's progress. Who are the player's foes, what do they want, what do they do, etc.? Is there a hierarchy to these foes? If so, who leads them? Concept art or images from other games will help give a feel for these foes.

COMBAT

How does combat work? How does the player battle forces inimical to their quest? (It's OK if combat does not fit the theme of your game, but be sure to tell us what characters or objects oppose the player's quest and how they overcome them.)

OBSTACLES

What inanimate challenges will the player encounter in your game?

OBJECTS, ITEMS, WEAPONS, ETC.

What inanimate objects can the player pick up or otherwise interact with? How do those work? Any parts of the environment that are interactable, detail them here.

REPLAYABILITY

How replayable is your game? What makes it replayable? If it isn't, try to make it so.

THE GAME WORLD

Tell us about your game world here. Fill in all sections as completely as possible. Add other sections if your game calls for them.

ENVIRONMENTS

Describe the environments the player will encounter in your game. Concept art and/or images from other games could help convey this.

KEY LOCATIONS

Describe any key locations in your world, places where vital parts of the story occur.

GAME FLOW

How does the PC experience your game world? How do the world's locations connect? Include the order in which the player encounters the sections of your game world. Note: Make sure the connections between areas are either logical or make sense within the context of your story!

INTERACTIVITY

What can the player do with your game world? How do they interact with it? List some examples of interactive objects, items, and locations here.

TRAINING

Is there a training level/area built into your game? If so, describe it here. If not, how does the player learn the controls and how to play? Does the training level also serve to familiarize the player with the game world and their PC?

MAP/LAYOUT

Describe the layout of your world here—how the levels, environments, or areas of your game world connect. Include a map(s) or image(s) showing this layout.

ART STYLE/AESTHETICS

What is the look and feel of your game? What atmosphere do you hope to create for the player? Give some visuals of the environments in which your story and game will occur.

Note: This section must include either original concept art or images/screenshots/concepts from other games that show the art style you're aiming for. Create sub-sections here as needed.

USER INTERFACE/CONTROLS

How does the player interact with your game world and its characters, items, and environment? What information and capabilities do you provide the player as they are playing?

INTERFACE

What information will you display on-screen for the player? Include a sketch of the UI during gameplay.

MENUS

What menus and capabilities do you provide the player (e.g., Inventory, Journal, Equipping/Loadout)? These should all be functions that enhance the player's experience. Include a sketch or image of each menu you plan.

MESSAGING

How does the game world convey information to the player? Is it via dialogue, text messages, verbal notifications, images and effects splashed onto the screen, etc.?

MUSIC AND SOUND EFFECTS

Tell us about the audio component of your game design. Keep in mind that audio works with the visuals, story, and gameplay to help create a unified theme for the player experience.

MUSIC

Describe the general style of the music for your game, the atmosphere you're trying to create, and the effect you hope the music has on the player. For each distinct area of your game, give suggestions as to the mood/ atmosphere the music should convey.

SOUND EFFECTS

Give us an idea of the kinds of events, player/NPC actions, and so on that will trigger sound effects in your game. Also list unique ambient sounds (background sounds) for each distinct area of your game, to convey the feel of that area (e.g., machinery and truck sounds in an industrial area).

Quest 6—Initial Digital Prototype

It's time to implement the game design plans you've made! Pre-production planning is over and now it's time to create your game. This prototype can be created as a solo project or on a small team.

For this assignment, turn in the initial playable prototype of your digital game (in Scratch, Twine2, RPGMaker, etc.). Don't worry too much about how things look at this stage—concentrate on getting gameplay into your game.

Quest 7–9—Playtesting and Revision

Each week, bring to class a noticeably better version of your game world— larger, with more content, and with increasing polish. Your game will be playtested by classmates every week. They will supply feedback that will help you improve your game world.

Quest 10—Final Digital Prototype

This quest calls for the final version of your digital game. Use the feedback received over the last few weeks to make your game as complete and polished as possible.

Quest 11—Devolver Project Proposal

The Devolver project involves students getting together in teams of 3–4 and picking a digital game to "devolve" into an analog version of that game. This requires students to analyze the mechanics of the original game, decide what players love about it, and then figure out how to replicate those mechanics in the analog version of the game.

In this quest, each student will submit a proposal for the Devolver project their team will work on for the rest of the semester. Each proposal should contain the following information:

- The name of the digital game the team is converting into an analog game.

- Some basic information about that digital game—what genre it's in, when published, etc. (1–2 paragraphs).

- The core game mechanics you have identified in the digital game that you plan to carry over into your analog game's design, and how you plan to convert them to analog form.

- What type of analog game (e.g., board game, card game, RPG, etc.) your team will create.

- Components you expect your game to have—board, cards, tokens, money, etc.

- Which member of team will be responsible for which elements of the game.

Quest 12—Initial Devolver Prototype

This quest begins the playtesting of each team's Devolver prototype. Teams are responsible for bringing a playable version of their game to class. It is understood that these games will be rough works-in-progress; just make sure that there's something significant for classmates to play and give feedback on. Then bring a better version for the next class.

Be sure to bring:

- At least two printed copies of your game's rules! This is the primary component of your game's UI—it needs to convey the game's "story" and rules to players.

- A rough version of any game board, card sets, etc. that are needed to play your game.

- Any dice or other pieces needed.

Quests 13–14—Playtesting and Revision

Each week, bring to class a noticeably better version of your game. It will be playtested by classmates every week. Their feedback will help you continue improve your Devolver game.

Quest 15—Final Devolver Prototype

In the last week of class, turn in the final version of the Devolver game you've been working on for the last few weeks. There will be one final round of playtesting, for students to give you a last set of feedback.

Quest 16—Reflection Paper

See the final assignment in the Narrative Design I class above.

SENIOR OVERVIEW ASSIGNMENTS

This class is only for students of senior standing. They are guided through the process of creating a capstone project, one that showcases all the skills they've learned in school and that is aimed directly at the career they want in the game industry.

Quest 1—Initial Milestone Map

The first assignment in this class is to lay out your plans for the project you'll create this semester. This project should be the culmination of all your work here at Webster, showcasing everything you've learned. It should also be aimed directly at the job you hope to get in the game industry and the career path you want to follow.

The document that you submit will be the initial version of your project's Milestone Map (MM). Read the instructions below and use the sections listed as guidelines for the organization of your MM.

Note that it is expected that each student's initial MM will require a revision over the following week.

GAME4620—MILESTONE MAP INSTRUCTIONS

This document will outline your plans for the entire semester, culminating in the completion of your Capstone project.

Your MM will consist of the following sections (use these sections as a template for your MM submission on 9/1).

Header—Give your project a title here. Also mention if you are working with anyone on this project.

Overview—A few paragraphs summarizing your goals and plans for this project. This should give the reader a solid idea of what your project is about and your end goals. Include player/audience impact, the experience you want to invoke.

Stages—In outline form, list the stages your project will follow, from inception to completion. If this is a cooperative project, tell what parts of each stage are your responsibility.

Elements and Assets—Either within the stages above or in a separate section (whichever best fits your project), list the pieces that are needed to complete each stage.

Weekly Task List—As a refinement of the "Stages" section, provide a bullet-pointed list of what you plan to accomplish each week of this semester. This is your initial road map from project start to completion.

Final Product—Give a clear, concise idea of the end product of your efforts in this class. What do you expect to end up with?

Assessment—How will this capstone project help you in your intended career? What skills do you want to showcase here? Be specific.

It will benefit you greatly to be as specific as you can in your MM. This is a commitment you are making to yourself. Make a detailed plan and work hard to stick to it.

Work during the semester to keep your MM a living document. Update it regularly with changes in your plans and progress toward your end goal. Use it as a tool for self-analysis, to see how you're progressing toward completion. This revised doc will also be turned in midway through the semester, to officially update your plans and note any changes to your original intent.

Quest 2—Revise Milestone Map

Use the comments your classmates and instructor made on your initial MM to help drive your revision. Any additional information requested should go into the revision you submit this week. This is essentially the planning/pre-production for your senior project, the road map that will drive its development, so details are good!

Quest 3–7—Project Presentations

Each week, each student makes a presentation during class. This is to show the class the progress that you've made on your project over the past week. The presentation should be done either in presentation software (Prezi, PPT, etc.) or in the app in which the project is being developed (Maya, Unity, etc.).

The first presentation should mostly show us what you plan to do over the course of the semester. Each subsequent presentation is expected to show more of the actual work you've accomplished as well as what's to come.

In general, organize your presentation around the following elements:

- A brief overview of your project.

- Your plan for completing it by the end of the semester.

- What you have accomplished over the past week.

- The current state of your project.

- What you plan to accomplish over the coming week (and showcase in your next presentation).

These presentations also serve the purpose of making students comfortable speaking to a group about themselves and their work. This is excellent practice for job interviews. To that end, students are expected to work on the following:

- Look their audience in the eye.

- *Not* read off a script.

- Make their presentation engaging and interesting.

These are skills that may not be natural to you at the start of the semester, but we will work on them each week.

The audience (your classmates and instructor) has work to do here as well. After each presentation, students should ask questions and make suggestions to the presenter. This will form part of your Participation grade in this class.

Quest 8—Mid-Semester Update of Milestone Map

Remember the MM you created in the first couple weeks of class? Time to revisit it. This quest asks you to return to the last version of your MM and update it.

- Adjust to reflect what you've done so far.
  - Note where you're ahead and where you're behind your initial expectations.
- Assess if you are on target, ahead of target, or behind (from initial MM).
- Break down rest of semester, what you'll accomplish every week.
- State what you expect to end up with, adjusting for work done thus far and expected effort to come.
- Leave time for polish!

Quests 9–14—Project Presentations

Students continue to present the state of their senior project every week, as outlined in Quests 3–7.

Quest 15—Final Project Presentation

This is where you show the end result of all your efforts. Give us an overview of the process and history of your project, from your starting plans to the final product. Talk about the problems you encountered, challenges you overcame, etc.

Quest 16—Reflection Paper

See the final assignment in the Narrative Design I class above.

Index